TRUTH AND IMAGINATION

The Universes Within

Frederick Sontag

University Press of America, ® **Inc.**
Lanham • New York • Oxford

University Press of America,® Inc.
4720 Boston Way
Lanham, Maryland 20706

12 Hid's Copse Rd.
Cummor Hill, Oxford OX2 9JJ

Printed in the United States of America
British Library Cataloguing in Publication Information Available

ISBN 0-7618-0921-X (cloth: alk. ppr.)

™ The paper used in this publication meets the minimum requirements of American National Standard for information Sciences—Permanence of Paper for Printed Library Materials, ANSI Z39.48—1984

For
Those who, by Grace, are gifted to discover
a new life of the spirit that lies beyond their
brush with physical death.

and for Brother
Barbara

Friends over
the years.

With love

Tal

Blake believed many of the ills of
the world result from a loss of
imagination and an unwillingness
to cultivate human energies in
freedom.

John Beer in <u>William Blake</u>, 1757-1927,
Profile Books, Windsor England, 1982, p.35.

Like all kids, we not only fooled
around with our toys, we changed
them. ... This impulse to make a
toy do more is at the heart of
innovative childhood play. It is
also the essence of creativity.

Bill Gates in <u>The Road Ahead</u>.
Viking Penguin, New York, 1995, p.2.

...without emotion there is no
imagination. p. 179
...emotion is the ground of
creation; it makes creation
possible. p. 222
...out of emotion the new arises. p.226

James Hollman in <u>Emotion</u>.
Northwestern University
Press, Evanston, 1964.

TABLE OF CONTENTS

PREFACE: Blake on the Origin of Creativity and Understanding

The finalized world of a new future, which the Modern Age foresaw, has so little come to pass that it is now hard for us to conceive how they could have projected it, save for the genius of imagination. As that era began, Modern science was exploding, mathematics changing; democracy was coming and the guarantee of universal human rights was foretold, utopias unlimited projected, religion outmoded and abandoned. Promethian man was to take fire from the gods and institute revolutionary, and thus radical, progress heretofore not possible.   Education could become universal, enlightenment extended; medicine was to produce miracles of bodily healing; and psychiatry would replace priests and so release the human spirit from internal suffering-- at last. Man, and soon women, would come into their own, once the power of ultimate control passed to them.

Blake, as we know, was a visionary-- too much so for his own time. 'Imagination', you might say, was for him the final human achievement.   And so he would, one might think, rejoice over the Modern Mind's vision of the future.   Yet, as the century closes with the aims of Modern Philosophy now lying in ashes all about us, it is long past the time to ask: What went wrong; why was the vision not fulfilled? Or to put the crucial question another way: Why would a visionary like Blake, who saw imagination as the soul of man, not have been swept away by the Modern Vision too? Let us list some of the key concepts that dominate Blake's poetry and writing to see if they help to reveal the Modern World's Achilles heel. Did the fault lay just where the Moderns thought they were invulnerable?

Stephen Sondheim was once being interviewed about his musical career. When asked what his favorite word was, he at first whirled around in his chair, but then after a pause he replied: "But I have so many favorite words," as must be true of any lyricist or poet or writer. However, after a moment more of thought, he replied: "pioneer". Anyone who knows the tradition-breaking quality of Sondheim's musical-lyrical creations will understand his choice. We used to venerate the pioneer's who sped America's development Westward away from the colonies, although now this story seems more likely to bring forth apologies rather than idolization. Our industrial giants and railroad builders certainly were also pioneers, just as much as those who ventured forth in covered wagons into the largely unknown. However, we have at times also celebrated our pioneers of the mind, artistic creators, inventors, actors and movie makers, writers of The Powerful Word, whether human in origin or divine in inspiration.

How, we need to ask, does one become so powerful in vision and expression, so driven as to pioneer creatively in any field? We know that the answer cannot lie with the average or with the ordinary, and certainly it does not come simply from our common sense experience. This question is intimately connected with the notion of 'truth'. For if we seek to appropriate truth, we know that it is more likely to be found in the unusual than in the simple, in the complex more than in the unitary, although many did once think it was to be found there. As the age of democracy dawned, we came to trust the common man more than the king, and for democracy's continuation we probably still must do so. But where insight into the secrets of our human existence is concerned, such truth may very well lie hidden from ordinary vision. If so, we are required to seek out the visionary, especially if he or she holds the key to our inner life which we need to discover.

Do we require the extraordinary power of the gifted in order to gain insight into the obscurity of our soul, and neither Freud's confident Rationalism nor the statistics of the Social Scientist? If so, both our human nature and our future may actually come more alive in the theoretical physicist's obscure speculation than in the single theory drafted by some scientific finalist in our last centuries. One must imagine worlds not visible to the eye, although perhaps 'real' in Plato's sense; these in fact may be more insight producing, and so perhaps far more 'real', than any empirical perception could be. If so, to seek simplicity in language and to try to reduce the meaning of obscure or complex terms to clarity, may be to trivialize a potentially powerful language, more so than if we follow a charismatic or a messianic leader--however much we can be led astray.

We did of course hope to solve our philosophical, linguistic, and personal problems by Rationalistic reduction. But does that now turn out to have been an odd hope, once viewed in retrospect, given both the depth of human perfidy and the heights to which the rare creative artist can reach? The ordinary must remain the ordinary, alas, much as we celebrated it by praising the arrival of democracy in the Age of the Common Man. Yet, we need not leave all universal understanding behind, at least where insight into today's complex, uncertain, and shifting world is concerned. Even Wittgenstein, who sometimes was mistakenly thought to make ordinary language the-be-all-and-end-all of philosophy, knew painfully well that, outside whatever certainty we might establish, lay the mystical-beyond. As we enter our new century, let us then turn back to locate the extra-ordinary in human imagination and then explore it as an uncertain passage to truth.

One example of the change, which took place from the first part of the twentieth century to the last part of those one hundred years, is the argument on my campus over Pomona College's motto: "Our tribute to Christian Civilization." Founded by Congregationalists, those successors to the New England Pilgrims, they saw, even in the California desert in 1887, that their work was to build up a college as their part in the effort to bring a 'Christian' civilization into existence. As the century ends, most students and faculty at Pomona are largely secular, whereas early in its centennial history most would have belonged to some Protestant (or Catholic) group. Thus, today the College motto often seems narrow and unacceptable to the non-religious. Yet they probably do not realize the secular utopianism, that vision so important in the country's founding, which inspired Pomona's founders too.

Except for colleges established by missionaries abroad, no country has the number of private colleges and universities that we have in the United States. Land grant and state universities came later to the scene. Education was not neglected in our era of pioneers; quite the opposite. The democratic principles of both church and state demanded near-universal education as a condition for self-government and successful democratic rule. Harvard was founded to train enlightened clergy, and also laymen who could respond to their minister at the same level on which the clergy spoke, and who had the mental skills necessary to interpret the Bible for themselves. The early and wide-spread antipathy in the U.S. toward Roman Catholics was partly due to the perception that they were not educated to be independent thinkers on either religious or secular matters but rather obeyed prescriptions given by Pope and king.

Pomona College, then, was founded in the same wide spread optimism and conviction of its time: that we had left distant and troubled lands behind in search of freedom and independence and that we would build a fresh civilization on this sparse continent as our portion toward establishing a new order in the world, "a city set upon a hill," a beacon to other nations. Such optimism, if not arrogance, has both attracted and repelled visitors from abroad for as long as America has held world attention. Thus, today's students need find no religious provincialism in Pomona's motto but rather should ask themselves whether they still share its utopian optimism regarding our ability to transform both ourselves and our human ways. The pursuit of universal education is a critical factor. This question is at issue in the whole land today: Can the U.S. fulfill its promise? Or have circumstances changed so drastically that we can no longer hope to rise to new humanitarian levels under our own guidance?

Oddly enough, as we will argue, the "democratic" notions of truth which created "empiricism" as a philosophical doctrine may have to go. Perhaps we counted too much on creating a united and a universally agreed populace, whereas now we must look more toward freeing the creative few to lead us, no longer the masses rising up from below ground level. Democratic theory can still remain dominant, since on the other hand no class or race or sex or economic position should offer to bring our future hope into being by itself. We need to look for imagination and inspiration today, wherever we can find it, both now and in our future. Perhaps we can only hope, not to transform ourselves by some universal agreement about truth, but simply to say that we will still try to offer every opportunity for inspiration and hold ourselves open to follow any new avenue which such rare voices announce, even if some prove to be misguided Pied Pipers. Some do run amuck by following an aberrant inspiration; yet we no longer have any choice but to take that risk.

Acknowledgements

Kris Kristofferson and I disagree over whether I suggested that he read William Blake while he was at Oxford on his Rhodes, or that he told me he had discovered "this poet" whom I should read. In any case, that discovery led, many years later, to this vision (or version) of truth.

Many thanks to Damon Tomeo, who prepared the MS for publication.

I. EXPLORING THE WORLDS WITHIN THE MIND

For our guidance in the 21st Century, should we turn to William Blake and not to the "main line" philosophers whose thoughts from England and Scotland and Ireland seem to have guided us for so long? As we know, Blake was a maverick in his own time; his "far out" thoughts were hardly popular. No Pilgrim landed at Plymouth Rock quoting Blake. No framer of the U.S. Constitution, The Declaration of Independence or The Bill of Rights quoted Blake on human rights. If we want to explain the struggle to establish universal human rights and to found democracies, Blake is not our man. But when democracies either rise up anew or fail each day, or perhaps more important grow dull and lethargic, or when religions lose their power to inspire-- to what can we look to revive our flagging spirit? The Common Man, so much touted, cannot do it. We need to turn away from sense experience, and even from any rigid Rationalism, to seek our inspiration from the worlds within the mind.

You can reply, and rightly so, that the human mind often strays afar and dwells too many times in far-out worlds, many of which are not in any way beautiful and some of which are perhaps even terrifying. Absolutely so. In our quest for the new vision in which Blake specializes, discrimination, balance, sensitivity, a sense of transcendent values and of new worlds-- these are absolutely crucial if we are not to get lost and drift in the dark caverns of our minds as so

1

many do. Thus, we search for The Messiahs of the Mind, the Prophets Within, for those who can lead us to a new vision by their verbal/artistic expression. These refresh us because they are the opposite of the stale, and they can renew us because they are more constructive than terrorist rage. True inspiration allows life to expand, not contract; it enable us to see/to explore visions which our individual souls might not discover on their own.

We know that Blake did not write systematic treatises on 'truth' as many philosophers might; nor did his writing proceed as Hegel would have liked, that is, by dialectical progression. He was, after all, primarily a poet. His essays and drawings are poetic in quality. Thus, if we want to catch his vision of truth, we need to discover how we might both explore and appraise his words of insight against what other philosophers have advised us as our best approach to truth. We will do this below by commenting on his suggested themes (in alphabetical order, for simplicity). Then we will see if anything can be drawn together from all of this by way of a new understanding for our insight into 'truth'. Yet, is Blake really a philosopher, or does it distort him to approach his writings in that way? Certainly he is a 'philosopher' in the classical sense of being a lover of wisdom, not claiming himself to be wiser than all but only to be a seeker. He approaches insight with passion, yet never asserts its possession as his exclusive right, life's questions being more important than any claim to final answers.

We must look to the worlds within the mind, rather than to those without, as so many Moderns did following what they thought would be empirically based sense experience or a final triumph of Rationalism. In Our New Century we need to turn in a different direction in order to find the inspiration of imagination. It is clear that not all we either see or explore, in the vastness of the worlds that lie potentially within the mind, is creative, much less that we know how to approach these strange lands. Empiricism hoped to provide a universal agreement on "one world" which we could all unite to explore. Descartes turned within himself, true enough, but as a Rationalist he expected to find there a world clear and distinct, guaranteed to him by a God of similar quality. Freud, who followed Descartes and Spinoza in their approach, thought that all in any human mind, even that which did not now conform to rational understanding, would eventually be straightened out by an exploration into our individual, and thus really uniform, biographies.

(1.) Art

"Art can never exist without Naked Beauty displayed."

The Laocoon, p.776[1]

We recognize that such a comment is at least partially true. Why, then, is the body so often covered, even if attractively so? Perhaps Art aims to reveal the naked body and is the symbol of this apprehension. In all Art, we see something that we know exists but do not regularly see displayed openly. Truth also has an aesthetic component, so that it is hard to portray except in an artistic rendering. And Blake claims that raw beauty can be expressed poetically where prosaic words are not useful. We must accept risk in our search for progress in perception. To do that we need something to reveal, to show forth, a naked beauty which we know exists but seldom see directly.

(2.) The Art of Invention

"To imitate I abhor... The art of Invention, not of Imitation. Imagination is My World."

Public Address, p.600.

The Empiricists wanted to limit us to our sensations in their hope to achieve universality; the Rationalists wanted us confined by our common reason. Both approaches to truth were either devoid of passion or sought to make us so. If we are to invent, which seems to be the very key to success in the 21st century, we must first reject the search for an intellectual universalism. Some minimal agreement may lie along that way but also perhaps our mind's stagnation. True, our inventive imagination is often bizarre. We will never reach a calm, universal agreement via inspiration, but it may now be the only way for us to venture into a productive future. Certainly, we know that

---

[1] *The Complete Writings of William Blake*, Ed. G. Keynes, The Nonsuch Press. London, 1938. All pages reverences in this section are to this edition.

using the sense experiences we all have will not lead us to creative
invention, because that does not come from the ordinary, the already
accepted. We seek something new, visions as yet unknown.

"None but the Blockheads Copy one another. My
Conception & Invention are on all hands allow'd to
be Superior."
Ibid., p.601.

To do what everyone else has done gets us nowhere, neither
in physics nor in mathematics nor in philosophy nor in religion. Only
the Empiricists thought otherwise. True, they helped to initiate the
establishment of democratic governments; but now we must learn to
distinguish that which allows every man and woman his or her human
rights but will still not block the constant invention we need in order
to   advance   a   democratic   state   against   all   repressive
political/intellectual regimes. Democracies, universal orders which
protect the rights of all, these were and still are "a giant step forward
for mankind". But now they must not be allowed to block that
advance which comes only by the individual, by particular, invention.

"I must Create a System or be enslav'd by another
Man's. I will not Reason & Compare: my business is
to Create"
Jerusalem, p.629.

Both Empiricism and Rationalism wanted us to "reason and
compare" and for a good purpose: to try to find a base that would
support common agreement among all human beings. Unfortunately,
they assumed a greater commonality among all cultures than probably
can ever exist, and certainly they were too simplistic in their notions
about the problem of intellectual and human complexity. We should
"reason and compare" when that seems appropriate, but Blake wants
us to know that invention and creation do not lie along that path.
Hegel, of course, wanted to unite all thought and all cultures in one
system, i.e. his. But such a vision seems to fade before an ultimate
plurality in thought and action and so seems unlikely to materialize.
Thus, we must, each one of us, create something for ourselves or be
enslaved by another's vision. Nature's created order does not seem to

have been based on a unitary scheme. Finality comes only by the effort of individual minds, and even then only for the moment.

(3.) Bible/Religion

"Both read the Bible day & night,
But thou read'st black where I read white."
The Everlasting Gospel, p.748.

In a secular age, it is important to search out the sources of our valued democratic achievements, both in politics and in our creative advances. (Let us agree that all cultures are not creative and that even those which are cannot expect to sustain their level of achievement without constant care). How odd it would be if in fact democracies rest on religion and, in Blake's case, on "the Bible". Religions, of almost all types, tend to claim to be universally available, and it is often God who is said to raise all of us to one level, whereas by Nature we are quite various. Thus, if we eliminate the Bible and the Hebrew/Christian/Muslim tradition, is it the case that we risk the loss of both the democratic spirit and our creativity?

You reply: But not all religions are the same and many are far from democratic in spirit. True, so we must examine religions, both Christian and non, for their support of political democracies and democratic principles regarding basic human rights (such rights being far from 'inalienable'), plus their encouragement of imagination. Immediately, all "Natural Religions" would seem to be eliminated, since Nature however conceived is not in itself creative but actually is a depressant on creativity. Christianity and Judaism and Islam, like most religions, have been both repressive and creative. How can we explore all religious traditions so that we bring out the inspirational side of each? Clearly there can be no universal rule, only individual experience and appraisal. Yet, if we do not keep these traditions alive for our exploration, we lose all hope of finding in them our needed imaginative spark, as the art world attests by its careful preservation of every great work in our past. Out of past genius solidified new inspiration can, not must, arise.

(4.) Blind Hand

"For I Dance,
And drink, & sing,
Till some blind hand
Shall brush my wing."
*Poems from the Note-Book and,
Songs of Experience,* p.183 & p.213.

If there is one way the Modern Age did not envisage God, or the Natural World, it was as a "blind hand". Yet anyone who experiences the world's unexpected turns has much more the sensation of a blind hand unexpectedly brushing him or her than of a God who operates "the best of all possible worlds", as Leibniz ironically suggested in his fantasy. But note the rest of Blake's suggestion: That even if we are removed by some blind hand's brush, we may, until that time, still dance and drink. Plato might have liked such a suggestion, but in Modern Times that has not been much recommended as a way to truth or as a philosophy of life.

Does 'ecstasy', as the ancients might have called it, provide a better, even if erratic, insight than the sane and sober Puritans would have recommended? Those who follow dance and song, or those who listen to and watch those who perform it, often feel that they are not very inspired by the Natural world but are by the ecstasy of art. They must see and then convey insights which could not be presented in a less artistic way. Words, even those in Blake's poetry, are not dance and song, and yet under some conditions they may convey what song and dance have led him and others to express. If a blind hand will brush and still our wings, our lives cannot be fully understood simply from our own rational constructions. Contingency, accident, chaos and the unexpected do characterize our life and so must figure in any explanation of our life, else an excessive Rationalism distorts the realities of our existence.

(5.) Brotherhood

Jesus said: "Wouldst thou love one who never died
For thee, or ever die for one who had not died for thee

and if God dieth not for Man & giveth not himself
Eternally for Man, Man could not exist; for Man is Love
And God is Love."
Jerusalem, p.743.

Democratic theories, and all Communist theories, stress brotherhood and claim that this quality is important if democracies, whether Communist or constitutional, are to survive.   Yet if no common feeling exists among us, democracies cannot long exist. We need to ask: what in fact may (not must) create real brotherhood among those who are by nature disjointed and multiple?

Blake suggests that this requires not any ordinary sacrifice but the ultimate sacrifice which Jesus' death signifies.   God was significant to most of the Empiricists and to all of the Rationalists, since their religious piety tended (oddly enough) to signify the supremacy of Reason itself.   However, to achieve brotherhood in the 21st-century God must now symbolize something quite different to the laity, an aspect of divinity possibly more important for achieving brotherhood and for our inventive stimulation than a Rationalist God could be: a willingness to sacrifice, to give of oneself for another.   This is Blake's special poetic harness on a central Christian concept, it is true.   But we need to ask whether this attribute of divinity alone is capable of creating the sense of brotherhood necessary for democracies to survive.   Surely I do not feel brother to all mankind in some natural, universal sense but rather more a feeling of alienation or even resentment too often bordering on hatred.   Can a willingness to sacrifice alone create or sustain brotherhood/sisterhood?   "How odd of God to choose Jesus"-- or any one source for inspired unity that also both distinguishes and separates us one from another.

(6.) Capacity
"To be or not to be
    Of great capacity."
An Island in the Moon, p.57.

Blake is known for his emphasis on talent and thus on the mind's special capacity, which is not a democratic or a universal quality such that we can argue on that basis that human rights either can or ought to be respected. Blake is aware of the burden which great talent creates, but he stresses even more the danger of letting it lie fallow. If one tries to suppress latent talent, it becomes even more destructive than Freud's warning against sexual repression and its resulting traumas could ever be. To be gifted involves pressures that the ordinary person cannot realize. But each one must make-- only the individual alone can make-- the decision to develop or not to develop that capacity.

(7.) Chariot of Fire

> Bring me my Bow of burning gold:
> Bring me my Arrows of desire:
> Bring me my Spear: O clouds unfold!
> Bring me my Chariot of fire.
>
> I will not cease my Mental Flight,
> Not shall my Sword sleep in my hand
> Til we have built Jerusalem
> In England's green & pleasant Land.
>   *Milton*, p.481.

"Chariots of Fire" is now famous as the title of a film on religious conviction and Olympic runners. But few movie viewers hear the Scot Presbyterian choir sing "bring me my chariot of fire" or know its origins in Blake and in Biblical verse.

Then where, we have to ask, do we find a Chariot of fire that can lead us to inspire both ourselves and others? Certainly we now know that it can be found in neither of the great classical theories of the Modern Era, that is, Empiricism or Rationalism, since Kant who crowned that era thought that mathematics and physics were about to be completed in theory. At the end of the 20th century, we know that both of those fields, and all of scientific theory, were not about to be fixed but rather to explode. "Possible worlds" opened before the scientist's eye, not a relatively fixed Natural order that the Moderns thought would stabilize us all. Instead, we have been launched into

"The Worlds Within the Mind", or at least we are driven to seek those worlds which lay latent even in the uninspired mind.

How then, we are forced to ask, are chariots of fire connected to the vision of building Jerusalem in England? Recall the earlier mention of Pomona College's motto which reflects exactly the same aim: to build a new civilization derived from Christian inspiration, one which would avoid the negatives of older orders. According to Blake, this cannot be done until we are inspired by Chariots of Fire, either to win Olympic races or to build new societies. Of recent, we have all too often lost sight of the vision to build Jerusalem anew, the old Jerusalem now being too often more a source of destruction than of inspiration. True, we probably were too optimistic at the opening of the Modern Age, both about building new Jerusalems and about finalizing philosophy and science. But as we tried to build utopian societies and found that to be beyond our powers, as that century's work closes, have we also lost our capacity for invention?

What can we still do for our actually existing democratic societies? In spite of Communism's failure, much is possible if only we are constantly on guard. But what about the Worlds Within the Mind, the possible new worlds to be uncovered and discovered there? The physical world, that which is all too much in front of us, inspires us so little now. Can our mind, or at least the minds of some few of us who are adventuresome, ride in chariots of fire that explore the mind's depths? Those arenas are so much more vast than Freud's limited biographical perspective could envisage, although they are closer to Jung's mental worlds comprised by our total collective unconscious. That is, can we allow the inspired few to lead us, in our democracies, in our education, and in our art, so that our mutual dreams do not come to naught? Mr. Smith should go to Washington, but not without a vision of the people's good and not without finding a way to inspire others to pursue it. In a democracy, all teachers may be equal, but where creativity is concerned some few are more equal than all the others combined.

(8.) Contrarieties

> "Beneath the bottoms of the graves, which
> is Earth's central joint,
> There is a place where Contrarieties are
> equally true."
>
> *Jerusalem*, p.677.

Hegel and all logicians would not like to hear this, since Hegel's Dialectic requires the reconciliation of opposites, and every logician assumes that logic can comprehend all radical oppositions within a single order. On the other hand, if there is in fact a place within the mind where contrarieties are equally true, we should seek to find that juncture, since it might also be the source of our inspiration. Such a meeting point would have to exist outside Hegel's reconciling dialectic and remain untouched by any logic's rules. Yet if we seek truth, we might find it at a place outside all logic, particularly if truth lies in the exceptional rather than in the normal, which is not what the Moderns assumed to be true.

> "Do what you will, this Life's a Fiction
> And is made up of Contradiction."
>
> *The Everlasting Gospel*, p.751.

We are forced to ask: What if in fact this life, which the Modern World wanted us to take as our standard and so assure us of a universal truth accessible to all, what if this life is at its best more fiction than fact? Then, we have to get beyond the natural, empirical world in our thought or else be lost in fiction, not fastened on fact as we once hoped to be. And what if the contradictions we experience do not yield a dialectical reconciliation and advance (in the Modern world's vaunted phrase) 'Progress' but in fact drive us, at least the adventuresome few, to explore beyond the natural order to find that obscure place to which the worlds of the mind lead us.

(9.) Doubt

> "If the sun & Moon should doubt,
> They'd immediately Go out."
> *Poems from the Pickering Ms.,* p.433.

At first one might think that Blake wishes to eliminate all doubts, as Descartes tried to do. But consider the other option: Even the Natural world requires passion and conviction to keep its order from failing. God has demanded the steady exercise of commitment even where the maintenance of the Natural order is our aim, not some eternally fixed system as Modern Science once envisioned. Entertaining this suggestion actually goes further to explain the uncertainties which 20th century scientists have encountered than does a divinely pre-fixed system. The Moderns thought that Reason was the model to emulate in order to achieve our desired certainty. If doubt must constantly be overcome in order to keep any order steady, this explains our continual experience of Chaos and Complexity, more so than a divinely determined and fixed order could.

> Reason says 'Miracle'; Newton says 'Doubt',
> Aye! That's the way to make all Nature out.
> > > > ...Only Believe!
> > Believe & try!
> 'Try, try, & never mind the Reason why."
> > > > Epigrams,Verses..., p.536.

Observing the progress and the regress of human beings, Blake's admonishment to "Try, try" may be our key piece of advice. After all, the issue is not so much the possession of a startling raw talent as it is the question whether you will "Try, try", talent being plentiful but courage in the face of uncertainty rare. "Believe and try" is the key, since success is never observable or even really predictable in advance only in retrospect. Religion has not and should not have become as obsolete as Freud and others thought it would be, since belief is required to underwrite any attempt at insight. Without belief in ourselves and in the possibility of creating something new, we are all barren.

(10.) Enlightenment

> "For light does seize my brain
> With frantic pain."
> *Poetical Sketches*, p.9.

The movement which called itself "The Enlightenment" had the quaint idea that whole societies could rise and achieve a new level, that the new scholarly and scientific tools at our disposal, plus critical intelligence, would make it possible for us all to achieve higher levels of mental liberation due to the new trails being blazed. That movement did achieve a release for many. It even helped advance some societies as a whole, but it tended to take that newly achieved birthright too calmly. Now that we have advanced, not calmly but more by a seizure of the brain accompanied by odd pain, when 'light', that ancient metaphor for insight, does arrive, perhaps it feels more like a possession from outside ourselves rather than as our own achievement.

(11.) Envy

> "Wilt thou bring comforts on thy wings,
> and dews and honey and balm,
> Or poison from the desert wilds, from
> the eyes of the envier?"
> *Visions of the Daughters of Abion*, p.192.

Progress, all achievement, all invention, brings forth its admirers, its spur to advance; but it also inevitably opens us to the eyes of envy. Thus no advance, no introduced novelty, can arrive with singular applause. Just because of the created novelty detractors arise, regardless of success. But with optimism maintained, envy passes while the achievement remains--although only sometimes not always; and it often brings the seeds of discontent with it. So the new atmosphere is not without its complexities, never simply beautiful and serene. We want, we need, invention and imagination; but they do not, cannot, come unattached from envy.

(12.) Esoteric

> "What is Grand is necessarily obscure to
> Weak men. That which can be made
> Explicit to the Idiot is not worth my care."
> *The Letters*, p.793.

Just because Art requires that Naked Beauty be displayed, we know Blake believes truth to be esoteric, not exoteric. That is the rock on which Empiricism flounders: Truth is simply not out there for us all to see. The problem lies not in improving our normal means of perception or understanding, as the Empiricists and Rationalists suggested; the first question is how to reveal what is hidden to most and next how to express what can never be understood fully or directly by all. Symbol, and all indirect forms of expression, are the order of the day. The Philosopher of Imagination is brother to the Prophet. If measured by the accepted standards of the day, both should expect rejection, since a majority can seldom understand what is esoteric.

(13.) Evil

> "Active evil is better than passive good."
> Annotations to Lavater, p. 77.
> "Heaven & Hell are born together."
> Annotations to Swedenborg's Divine Love, p. 96.

One event gave the Modern World false optimism that it could achieve an advance over the past. This was the sometimes assumed belief (and it proved to be a belief, not a fact) that the evils of past ages, both human and social, had been or could be left behind. They believed: new ways of understanding could be secured which would be untouchable by human frailty. Not all went as far as Marx did to locate all evil and degeneracy in a class which could now be eliminated. But increased education and scientific progress did seem to guarantee that a new world was about to be born, one better and more in our control than the world's first birth in Eden. Yet if the good that is born is passive, Blake cautions us, then the action which evil represents may in fact be better, i.e., more sustainable.

All opposing worlds are linked. We can have a new heaven, even a Marxist classless society if you wish, but none can ever be separated from hell. We bring potential self-destruction with us into our every new creation. Utopias can be created, but not without their link to new possible destruction. It is not that Hell must necessarily come to us, but it is that its revival can neither be ignored nor prevented in any secure way. Devils are still made from rebellious and jealous angels. And also: Rebellion cannot be eliminated, since it is the necessary path to released imagination and thus truth. The road to truth is never singular but always dual and contradictory, in spite of all the traditions that long for unity and simplicity. In spite of much Western classical theology, God is complex not simple; the ample reaches of our mind's vast myriad worlds demand constant vigil if control is ever to be achieved or sustained.

(14.) Feeling

"I hate reasonings. I do everything by my feelings."
An Island in the Moon, p.50.

Blake put these words into the mouths of the Empiricists, and they often aim to enjoy what pleases. But feeling is perhaps even more significant for Blake. Hume in fact saw the weakness in the Empiricist's ignoring of feelings and himself moved to describe the power of emotion. However, Hume saw passion as thwarting the goal of empirical knowledge, not as itself a necessity for insight in our apprehension of truth. Emotion was rather an interference.

"Hang Philosophy!" Blake exclaims. "I would not give a farthing for it. Do all by your feelings, and never think at all about it."
Ibid., p.51.

So when we use Blake to advance philosophy, we must recognize his own views about how it often interferes with insight. Must we then throw out all philosophy if we want to follow Blake on the imagination's exploration of the worlds within the mind? Not necessarily, since Blake clearly had in mind his own country's more empirically oriented philosophy. We need to ask how poetry, in particular Blake's imaginative use of words, might move philosophy further from his negative image of it. In spite of Blake's advice, we know that, if not properly used, feelings can run amuck and be distracting rather than insightful. Heidegger recommended that philosophy must understand its similarity to poetry. So the key to its usefulness must be how feeling is channeled to that end. We all know Plato's image of passion as the force driving exploration, but also his recommendation that reason should exercise control.

Yet, for all of Plato's often overlooked concentration on passion as crucial to the mind's advance, Blake probably wants us to try a more venturesome approach than Plato's, one more risky and thus subject to loss. Must we, then, risk damage in order to explore? Is truth not really accessible to the cautious? Perhaps there are barriers to further advance that come with the level of enlightenment. If so, we must ask: Does our terror-filled age hide its secrets from obvious vision and demand, for the achievement to any new stage, the kind of breakthrough that only a daring imagination can provide? There may be both easier and more difficult times than ours when it comes to opening new approaches to truth. Too often we look at achieved insight, even Blake's. Just because it is there, its realization seems safe. But often we ignore the cost, and the unknown loss, which could be considerable. We do not fully recognize the power of feeling, both its necessity for real breakthrough and its danger for our disorientation.

(15.) Forgiveness

"What then did Christ Inculcate?
Forgiveness of Sins. This alone is the Gospel,
& this is the Life & Immortality
brought to light by Jesus."

The Everlasting Gospel, p.757.

In a time when all religions, and sometimes particularly Christianity, are thought to be regressive, we need to pay attention to Blake's own close association with religion. Of course, Jesus did recommend forgiveness, and this is not too much practiced in any world we live in, religious, secular, or even imaginative. If so we need to ask: Does forgiveness, as Blake sees it, have anything to do with imagination and the freeing of the mind for art and creativity?

How could that be, since forgiveness seems to be so much an odd and a rare religious phenomenon? Could it be that, since our minds in fact need release from the world before us, hatred and the continued blame attached to any offense ties our minds and our passions to the empirical world, rather than releasing us to explore other areas within the mind that are available to us--but not if the mind remains tied to negative passions. The major point to note is that the release of a driving passion is needed for discovery. Yet this is very difficult, perhaps impossible, if passion is tied to wounds and remembered wrongs. The creative person, or the one who would become possessed by such power, can be blocked by an inability to forgive. Jesus' admonishment is not so esoteric, if we really wish to discover truth, since only trivial truths come from the obviously empirical. What releases passion to creativity?-- not the world of sight and sound, nor even our internal worlds if bound by negativity.

(16.) Genius

"Ages are all Equal. But Genius is Always Above the Age."
Annotations to Reynolds, p.461.

Hegel, who saw World Historical figures like Nietzche's Superman as being above us all, still thought that the insightful leader was produced by his age, although the leader was on its cutting edge and so could forecast the future from it. Blake's suggestion is more radical than that. His innovations are above the age, and moreover no age is special or "more advanced" than another. The creative genius, the one who leads us to new truth, is not of the age, since real truths are new to their time. Such a person is not produced by his or her age, and so his or her vision cannot be produced from it. To be 'above' is to stand alone, to visualize what those engrossed in themselves or in their times cannot see. Historical study can be a detriment, which my be why so many creative people are educational drop outs.

"Go, tell them the Worship of God is honoring his gifts
In other men: & loving the greatest men best, each according
To his Genius: which is the Holy Ghost in Man; There is no other
God than that God who is the intellectual fountain of Humanity."
Jerusalem, p.738

Genius, insight, creativity cannot be, should not be, a matter of democracy. To discover God one must search out those who are divinely inspired in the day. We have to and should love those heroes, the creative few. Blake, thus, defines a new role for the Holy Spirit in the worship of God. "No inspiration, no possession by a Holy Spirit, no God, no source of intellectual creativity". This is Blake's motto.

(17.) God & Man

"But God is a man, not because he is so perceiv'd by
man, but because he is the creator of man."
Annotations to Swedenborg, p.90

Blake reverses the traditional argument for God. We do not argue from this world to the necessity of God as its creative source. The natural world is neutral, even often negative, where discovering divinity is concerned. We should argue to God from man, since our rare, but not universal, creative source demands an explanation. Plants and animals and even stars do not need a divine explanation. They simply came to exist. But the creative spirit in men and women, which often rises far beyond its humble source in human bodies, this elicits (not demands) a non-natural source to explain the fountains of creative expression which sometimes flow forth from our best.

> "I am in God's presence night & day,
> And he never turns his face away,
> The accuser of sins by my side does stand
> And he holds my money bag in his hand."
>
> *Epigrams*, p.558.

Blake has strong words for those who claim not to be able to find God. Just as the mystics have always found God immediately present, even if not so detected at all, Blake finds himself always in God's presence. We do not necessarily realize this, as the world's prevalent atheists attest. But the divine presence is there, because we must account for the bursts of creative energy which come forth from time to time, in any age or place. The natural course of history cannot account for this. Why are we not domesticated animals, content to have uniform thoughts and to be like all others as frogs are? Our discontent, our creative intuitions, although rare, indicate possible contact beyond our present natural home.

(18.) Holy Ghost

> What is the Divine Spirit? is the
> Holy Ghost any other than an
> Intellectual Fountain?
>
> *Jerusalem*, p.717

In the Christian tradition, we know that the Holy Spirit is given credit as the source of inspiration which allowed the formation of the Christian church. However, here Blake gives it an intellectual rather than primarily a spiritual twist. It spawns concepts as well as passion. Inspiration, for the philosopher or for the poet, cannot be wholly a matter of passion. It must form words into intellectual concepts so that they become a structure for us to build up to truth. And this power is not restrained or easily contained. Like the fountain, it overflows but can still lead to truth.

> "Go, tell them that the Worship of God is honouring his gifts
> In other men: & loving the greatest men best, each according

To his Genius: which is the Holy Ghost in Man; there is no
other God than that God who is the intellectual fountain of
Humanity."

Jerusalem, p.738

Divinity has not kept all its gifts but has distributed them,
although quite unevenly, and asks not so much to be worshipped, as an
otherworldly source of all, but to be recognized in the gifts exhibited
by those whom it has inspired. True, Christianity has normally been
thought to advise us to love all equally and democratically, but there is
nothing mentioned about all not being equally gifted and only some
inspired. Genius by definition cannot be equally distributed, but its
rare gifts should be used for the benefit of all equally.

As a divine light the Holy Ghost is not kept to itself by God-
in-Heaven but parceled out and lives present in some, but not in all,
men and women. There is an intellectual fountain which we recognize
by the creative gifts we see pouring forth from genius--when and
wherever we find this. Are you looking for God? Do you doubt
divinity's existence? Then look to the individual whom you find
provides an intellectual fountain, the source for our inspiration and our
admiration. God need not, cannot, be thought to be totally distinct but
rather to be totally "with us", as Christianity has proposed in its notion
of incarnation. But in this case, Blake asks us to look for divinity now,
here, around us, in its human embodiment. Like love, it simply
overflows its rare source within the mind.

(19.) Humility
God wants not Man to humble himself:
Humble towards God, Haughty towards Man,
This is the Race that Jesus ran
The Everlasting Gospel, p.750

Since God holds the secret of truth's location, one should be
humble toward so powerful and designing a source. Other men and
women are another matter. They are fellow pilgrims with us in our
pursuit of the endless unsolved questions and so, as a comrades with
us, we should be constantly aware of our mutually perilous pursuit.
Jesus is Blake's model. He was humble towards God, his source, but
not toward any who claimed to have the whole world in their hands

(check out the words of the Negro spiritual), when it is true that only God has the rare ability to judge and to command with finality. Men become arrogant only by thinking they have stolen fire from God.

(20.) Imagination

> "The Imagination is not a State: it is the
> Human Existence itself."
>
> *Milton*, p.522

    If this perception of Blake's is true, it is like the Neo-Plotinian discovery of the unity within the soul that links us to the One. This marks out the divinity we can find within ourselves and which can then draw us up toward simplicity and reunion. However, if the core of humanity in fact is not this unity and a tendency to withdraw from multiplicity but lies instead in a burst of creativity captured better by novel and creative suggestion-- then imagination becomes our key to God's perception and to uncovering our individual connection to divinity. But do we find all in agreement around this crucial core? No.

> "The world of Imagination is the world of Eternity. "
> *A Vision of the Last Judgment*, p.605

    As far as theology goes, Blake is perhaps most helpful to us in changing a conception of divinity which has been too long dominant, that of a fixed and complete and thus immovable God. This intransigent notion of divinity is found neither in the Jewish nor in the Muslim nor in the Christian scriptures. It comes rather from a metaphysics of completion-as-perfection; whereas in both Hebrew and Christian Scriptures what we face is a God who is constantly involved in new developments and thus is often in agony. Now Blake tells us that what we'll find in Eternity is a World of Imagination; far beyond Disney's conceptions or Star Wars' depiction. If creativity that sustains itself marks us at our best, how could we ever have decided to block God out of the most creative, if dangerous, side of human nature?

"For All Things Exist in the Human Imagination"
Jerusalem, p.707

Blake pulls a reversal on us, which is typical of poets and creative thinkers. Theologians from Augustine on down have piously placed every thought of every event in the divine mind, held eternally there, a completed script which we then act out in time. Now Blake tells us that All Things Exist in the Human Imagination. That divine attribute, so long admired, is really our own, or at least it exists among our most creative. Literally, we know that this finality which has been projected onto divinity cannot be true, since we do not see all things under the aspect of eternity, as supposedly God has programmed us to do. Our minds are often crowded, but not that crowded. Yet, when imagination falls on us in its full force, in a novel or in a manuscript or on canvas, the originator feels like a medium for a fullness of expression that is far beyond his or her own origin, thus turning the artist into a vehicle.

"And Earth & all you behold; tho' it appears
Without, it is Within,
In your Imagination, of which this World
of Mortality is but a Shadow." *Ibid.*, p.709

Today the empiricist aim has been reversed. They wanted to take the world without and agree upon it as a standard to give our every odd thought a reality test. But Blake tells us that it should be the other way around. What our senses perceive is but a shadow of something more real. This reminds us of Plato's shadows on the wall in the cave, which the prisoners (mere Empiricists?) took as reality. Imagination becomes the test for Reality, not simply sense experience. This does not say that everything we imagine is factual, but it does tell us where we have to begin to look for truth.

"The Spectre is the Reasoning Power in Man, & when separated
From Imagination and closing itself as in steel in a Ratio
Of Things of Memory, It thence Frames Laws and Moralities
To destroy Imagination, the Divine Body, by Martyrdoms & Wars."
Ibid., p.714

Now Blake turns Rationalism around from the Modern Era's celebration of it. Yet it is only dangerous when it runs amuck and is detached from Imagination. He might even have been thinking of the psychology of Leibniz' monad, that is, of a mind closed in upon itself and perceiving all things from within itself. Such is not our case, if and only if we do not lose touch with Imagination. Oddly, then, it is imagination which can keep Rationalism from deceiving us, not the other way around.
(Yet again)

> "What is the Divine Spirit?
> Is the Holy Ghost any other than an
> Intellectual fountain?"
>
> *Ibid.*, p.717

In most religious literature the Holy Spirit has been made out to be an inspiring spirit which founds new religions (Christian Science or Mormonism) by its power. But it has seldom been thought of as an Intellectual Fountain. If it can pour forth rivers of life and make us creative, then in that capacity it can more easily be seen to link the starved human intellect with a reviving creative spirit. Yet, if it is an "intellectual fountain", it can move the mind almost more than can the passions, whatever their role in imagination may be. This Holy Spirit is far from being fixed but instead communicates by overflowing. Thus, it explains the emergence of all that is strange but still attractive in religions by which we are so often moved, e.g., Seventh Day Adventists, the Amish.

> "Resounding from their Tounges in thunderous
>   majesty, in Visions
> In new Expanses, creating exemplars of
>   Memory and of Intellect,
> Creating Space, Creating Time, according
>   to the wonders Divine
> Of Human Imagination Throughout all the
>   Three Regions immense

> Of Childhood, Manhood & Old Age; &
>   the all tremendous unfathomable
>   Non Ens"
>
> *Ibid.,* p.746

    Had the author of *Genesis* had Blake's *Jerusalem* at hand, he might have given a much more imaginative account of the creation of man and the world, rather than the rather prosaic one we find recorded in that powerful myth.

    Why is it not conceivable that God's creation mirrors the upheavals and the visions of our imagination at its most prolific? We know now that we do not inhabit the only possible world but merely one of an unknown number of equally possible worlds. Given the explosion of expanses in mathematics and in physics (how could Kant have thought these fields about to be completed?), how can our later day, our 21st century vision of divine creation be less expansive than that of the theoretical physicist probing spaces never encountered by an Empiricist? Space and Time must be created according to Divine wonders, since the pioneer in science finds himself or herself on a constant space odyssey. There are then unfathomable Non Ens, not a neat and fixed natural order designed to give us a sense of security.

> "The Whole Bible is filled with Imagination and
>   Visions from End to End & not with Moral Virtues"
>
> "Jesus considered Imagination to be the Real Man..."
>
> "The perceptions of sense are gross."
>
> "By experiments of sense we become acquainted with the
>   lower faculties of the soul."
>
> "The Whole Bible is filled with Imagination and
>   Visions from End to End & not with Moral Virtues"
>   *Annotation to Berkeley*, p.774

    Perhaps nowhere more than here do we see Blake's opposition to Empiricsm, even Berkeley's more idealistic version. Of course, the Bible is filled with visions, so to attempt to appraise it by an ordinary form of experience is to misunderstand it. And if it is true that sense stimulates only the lower faculties of the soul, what can raise us to the best of the soul's potential? It is of course an exaggerated fact to say that Jesus considered imagination to be the real man, but if you meditate on the non-visual doctrine which he proclaimed, it could be that it could not then, and still cannot, be apprehendable by the unimaginative.

"The Eternal Body of Man is The Imagination, that is, God himself." (p.776)

This explains Blake a bit more, since Blake raises men to Gods, but significantly not on the basis of sense data. Spinoza raised man to God too, or at least he wanted man to do that for himself, whereas Blake is more clear that it is not so much in human reason as in imagination that man comes closer to God. Again, considering God as the world's creator, imagination must have played a major role in designing the vast alternatives and in choosing one path out of the many. Sense experience tells us little about such creative effort.

"What is Grand is necessarily obscure to Weak men.
    That which can be made Explicit to
    the Idiot is not worth my case."

"I feel that a Man may be happy in This World,
    And I know that This World Is a World of
    Imagination & Vision."
                                        Letters, p.793

At times Blake may seem almost as extreme as Nietzsche; yet it is not really so. Nietzsche is talking about power, and his Superman is a super-power-driven man. Blake is talking of vision and imagination, something sense experience does not offer to the ordinary viewer. This also takes strength, but it is a strength of the creative spirit, not power in the same sense that dominates our natural order; that which Nietzsche wanted to appropriate. Since the whole idea is to rise beyond the ordinary, we need a Super Man or Woman, yes, but not one of physical, political power. Happiness, then lies not in the control of the sheep-like following masses, as it might be for Nietzsche. It comes by accepting visions that exhalt.

> "There is a vast Majority on the side of Imagination or Spiritual Sensation."
>
> *Letters*, p.794

Odd that Blake should speak of 'majority' where spiritual sensation is concerned, since that would seem to be the province of the few. However, Blake feels that imaginative visions are really aimed at us all; most of us have just not yet been raised to that level. But we all could be, if we recognize the novel when it is presented, that is, if it speaks to and awakens our spiritual side. Sense experience might but seldom does this. Man is a true spiritual being for Blake, and so all depends on having a vision strong enough to inspire and to awaken that dormant capacity. Religion is key, in the sense of awakening the spiritual soul versus our rational/sensational capacities.

Clearly, imagination is a major and important theme for Blake, a latent capacity which he feels both the Rationalists and the Empiricists have either ignored or stifled. Of course, both of those traditions were looking for something more universally agreed upon, a common ground to which we could appeal in order to achieve unity in thought. Such is impossible in the case of vision and imagination, and yet Blake's whole point is that here lies both the center of our nature and the source of that inspiration which alone opens us to a new future. Certainty was a key goal of the Moderns, and this is the last thing possible where imagination is concerned-- because it can so easily go wrong.

More importantly, imagination allows us no immediate tests. Such can lie only in the future, and who knows how far into the future we must go to find confirmation. On this point Blake is much closer to Kierkegaard than to Nietzsche. The Superman's triumph will seem obvious in his day. But Kierkegaard said that we must make the future our standard, not some fixity of the past. And where the future is concerned, uncertainty of necessity abounds. Mistakes may be the order of the day and the results of our chance-taking are so not obvious for some time. Much depends on our strength to hold on to the future in the present and very little upon our grasp of the events of the past which led us up to our time. God, we know, has fixed neither his nature nor our future but has simply opened the soul's door to imagination and vision-- if one will risk and venture, which the majority can never do.

(21.) Inspiration

> "If Moses did not write the history of his acts, it takes away the authority altogether; it ceases to be a history & becomes a Poem of probably impossibilities, fabricated for pleasure, as moderns say, but I say by Inspiration."
>
> *Annotations to Watson*, p.390

Perhaps key to our understanding of truth-according-to-Blake is this complex notion of inspiration. Again, it is non-democratic; by definition it comes to the amazed few, who generally are surprised by its arrival upon their lives. And note Blake's contrast to history, that great projected avenue to truth of the 18-19th centuries. Inspiration lies neither in fact nor in history but rather in a poem of "probable impossibilities", a conjunction designed to thwart Modern notions of simple truth. Such inspirations as these are not idle dreams but rather are brought on by a rare inspiration.

Where, then, do we look for truth, if Blake warns us that inspiration comes not from simple facts now clarified, not even if by Hegel's dialectic, but arises by "probable impossibilities". Of course, Marx believes in the power of contradiction too. It drives his dialectic. However, it does not lead to inspiration for the favored few but to a universal conclusion for all, a "classless society" where all (who survive) are equal--as they most certainly are not now. Blake does not find truth in historical process. In fact, it arrives independent of its age's universal qualities, and it probably cannot, will not, be recognized by the masses. It involves a lonely factor, one not found in the adulation of the world's historical figures.

"Let the Bard himself witness. Where hads't Thou
This terrible Song?"
The Bard replied: 'I am inspired! I know
          it is Truth! for I Sing."
                                                  Milton, p.495

Philosophers do not normally burst into song or write poetry--
at least, it does not seem to be part of their professional function. But
if we are embarked on the quest for truth, that is, exploring the
questions more than formulating answers, words formed into poetry
and a voice driven to song, could these be the hallmarks of the arrival
of truth? We know, of course, that both poets and singers must be
inspired, since all verse and song is not the same and some shows the
mark of its inspired origin. Philosophers may write in prose and be
unable to sing, yet Truth might still spring from that source.

(22.) Jesus

"But Jesus is the bright Preacher of Life."
                                                  Jerusalem, p.718

Much as Kierkegaard uses the Christianity of his day and his
reaction to it as an instrument of philosophical reform in his outlook,
Blake reinterprets the role of Jesus to enhance his own themes.
Considering the dire words attributed to Jesus at times, not to mention
the agony of the Garden, the trial before Pilot, his crucifixion and his
disciples desertion, it is hard to see Jesus as "The bright Preacher of
life"-- except to see Jesus as an instrument of inspiration and his
paradoxical life as a challenge to our imagination to reinterpret his
chosen role. Everyone failed Jesus in his time. And even in its depths
he thought that God had deserted him too; his novelty was just too
much. But in time the power of his figure to stir our imagination can
"bring good things to life", as General Electric says.

"Did Jesus teach doubt? or did he
Give any lessons of Philosophy,

Charge Visionaries with deceiving,
Or call Men wise for not Believing?"
The Everlasting Gospel, p.756

Blake clearly uses 'philosophy' in at least two senses. One sense, as the British Skeptics might suggest, challenges us not to accept but to question. However, his other meaning for philosophy is closer to the visionary. Jesus, who stands as the symbol for our belief in the visionary, challenges us to believe in vision. Does this mean that Blake feels that every vision which comes to anyone is somehow true? Not at all. But he does want to say that the truth we look for may be located more in vision than in any empirical or historical fact. No vision in itself deceives. We alone do that by treating it as literal truth.

"What can this Gospel of Jesus be?
What Life & Immortality,
What was it that he brought to Light
That Plato & Cicero did not write?"
The Everlasting Gospel, p.758

As philosophers and poets do, and as Jesus did himself, Blake leaves it to each individual to explicate the exact statement of what the Gospel--any Gospel--means.   This is the advantage of the incompleteness that lies in the Gospel's themselves. The do announce as finished what cannot be final, but this open-ended quality is exactly that which the Enlightenment hoped to eliminate. Because Blake takes Jesus as a visionary, it is clear to him that Jesus brought something to light for us, however much it is still subject to misinterpretation. It is just not exactly clear what any Gospel is or how its truth can be brought to light. Ours is the work of response, and no uniformity is projected or even thought to be possible. Individual visions can be caught and perhaps passed on, but they are not, they cannot be, guaranteed.

(23.) Lamb of God

"Where is the Lamb of God?
where is the promise of his coming."

Milton, p.501

The 'Lamb' is, of course, a frequent way of referring to Jesus, but here again Blake catches the traditional note of stressing questions and not fixed doctrine. Christians perhaps too easily proclaim Jesus' coming, both then and now. But Blake knows that Jesus was never finally accepted then and still is not yet. We have to look for the Promise first; this question sets the Christian mood. That is one more of still-expected fulfillment, not of finalization. Given the division of opinion regarding Jesus' mission that remains, it is best to follow the mood of waiting-for-the-promise.

(24.) Liberty

"Let Liberty...
Enerve my soldiers; let Liberty
Blaze in each countenance, and fire the battle.
The enemy fights in chains, invisible
            chains, but heavy;
Their minds are 'fetter'd; then how can they be free?"

Poetical Sketches, p.18

Blake does not stress political liberty quite as strongly as many. There is a needed physical liberty, true. But he stresses a more important aspect, the freedom of the mind. Soldiers must fight to preserve it, but none whose minds are constricted can readily understand the freedom they need. Vision and inspirations, again, inspire the mind and thus free it from boredom, that mortal enemy of the final freedom of the human spirit.

(25.) Love

For Mercy has a human heart,
Pity a human face,

And Love, the human form divine,
And Peace, the human dress.
Songs of Innocence, p.117

Love is of course another major theme for Blake, both in its traditional place as the source of the poet's inspiration and in his use of Christianity as a revelation of the ideal for human nature. Not by any means are humans all good; almost the opposite. Thus, love creates surprise and excitement when it appears, just because we take it as the divine in human form.

"Love seeketh not itself to please,
"Not for itself have any care
"But for another gives its ease
"And builds a heaven in hell's despair."
Poems from the Notebook, p.162

These much quoted lines are clearly Blake's poetic rendering of St. Paul's famous description of ideal love as not self-concerned. But he goes on to see the other less ideal side of love; we might call it Passion, as Sondheim painted it in his musical by that name. As such, Passion can build a hell in spite of heaven, whereas love that seeketh not itself does the opposite and can build a heaven in hell's despair. When we "bind another to its [our] delight," that creates not freedom and heaven, but rather a hell in a place where hope might have been.

And thine is a Face of a sweet
        Love in despair,
And thine is a Face of mild sorrow &
        care
And thine is a Face of wild terror and fear
That shall never be quiet till laid on
        its bier.
Poems from the Pickring Ms., p. 429

The coupling of love and terror shows Blake's lack of Romanticism. Our inspirations always come mixed--and perhaps so much the better for our insight. Love alone is not penetrating enough to yield truth. Terror and fear disturb our quiet, and without that we become still. Even before we reach our grave, we can lose the needed restlessness that keeps us from quietude.

> Seek Love in the Pity of others' Woe,
> In the gentle relief of another's care,
> In the darkness of night & the winter's snow,
> In the naked & outcast, Seek Love There!
> *Ibid.*, p. 436

We usually think that we find love by satisfying our own interests, but Blake suggests that it is best found in the "pity of others' woes". This is the opposite of what we usually believe, since we expect love to lie in the gratification of our desires, or at least in Plato's sense in our love of some beautiful object. Blake of course is suggesting a Christian notion of love, the concern for the underprivileged. We should relieve pain, he suggests, but not our own--if our love is genuine. Dark night and the outcast, that seems a strange place to seek love.

Could it be that Blake has a clue to the unusual, not the obvious, source of love? We think of erotic satisfaction; Blake thinks of the relief of suffering. We admit that we often encounter trouble when love lies only in our self gratification. Could Blake be right that love is most genuinely found in the outcast? If so, this would explain why hedonistic satisfaction so often has trouble sustaining itself beyond the moment. Does the soul in fact grow when it secures another's need more than its own? This would put love in another mode, not in the common form of satisfaction. Again, truth would lie in the unusual and in the different, not in the ordinary and the common.

> "Our Quarrels arise from Reasoning..."
> "Without Forgiveness of Sin, Love is Itself
>   Eternal Death."
> *To the Deists*, p.699

In this statement Blake could not be more opposed to the Rationalists. Spinoza, Descartes, Leibniz--all believed that Reason leads to solutions and thus to peace. All quarrels, on that account, are the result of a failure to Reason. As Blake sees it, Quarrels in fact can arrive from Reasoning. The issue, of course, is whether Reason in itself leads to unity. But, if Reason is not itself unitary, then perhaps it could not reconcile us to each other but rather lead to diversity and difference. If so, Reasoning alone will not solve our conflicts, only forgiveness can, since without that we are simply locked into oppositions. "Love is itself Eternal Death."

Nothing could be more opposed to a Romanticism which sees love as always leading to beauty and peace. But what if, as Blake suggests, love itself actually can lock us into Eternal Death? Then only forgiveness, Blake argues, could release us from this irony. Love, then, is not a solution to all tensions, as Romantic thought suggests but can just as easily lead to death without release. Given some of our recent experiences with unbridled love, it might seem that this can be true, that love in itself is no solution to human problems but actually is often the occasion for division. Nor can Reason solve our difficulties as we had hoped. Forgiveness becomes the key.

> Jesus said: "Wouldst Thou love one
>   who never died
> For Thee, or ever die for one who had not
>   died for Thee?
> And if God dieth not for Man & giveth not
>   himself
> Eternally for Man
>   Man could not exist; for Man is Love
> As God is Love; every kindness to
>   another is a little Death
> In the Divine Image, nor can Man exist but by Brotherhood."
>   *Jerusalem*, p.743

Blake again makes love a more complex phenomenon than our romantic tendencies paint it. In his mind it is linked to death, just as it was for Jesus. So finding love is not a simple matter of bliss. One must often die for another in order to verify love, which Jesus did. We should never forget that, with Jesus, love and death are forever linked together. God in fact does this eternally, else man could not exist. Our life depends on God's willingness to die, and life does not begin as some creation fable that postulates an at first perfect existence. Man is only love as God is love, so that to understand ourselves and our attempts to love, we have to understand God's willingness to sacrifice. All else is playing selfish games with love. Kindness involves a "little death", because kindness when it is real is not easily given but instead often requires sacrifice. We do not exist alone, in spite or our attempts at independence. Instead, we live fully only in brotherhood.

(26.) Mercy

> "Mercy Pity, Peace
> Is the world's release."
> *Poems from the Notebook,* **p.164**

In the age past, which was one of our own devised utopias, we thought of a hundred ways to seek our own release. Blake wants to tell us that mercy is the only avenue of release, whereas we have in the course of our history thought of many other sources. Pity has not often been considered as the road to peace, but Blake charts a different path for us, one less obvious in a Rationalist age. We have thought we could negotiate peace by mutual discussion. Blake tells us that Mercy and Pity are our only hope of achieving a change in our life of constant conflicts. Given the terrors and hostilities of current oppositions, nothing now could seem a less likely avenue to peace than rational discussion, since Reason can plead for individual divisions and recommend destruction just as easily as it can promote peace. Again, Without Forgiveness of Sin, Love is Itself Eternal Death.

We have also thought that love, as an instinctive impulse, could lead to human resolution. Blake tells us that, without forgiveness of sins, love actually can be eternal death and not release at all. If this is the case, we have placed too much hope for resolution on the emotion of love. It is, in fact, useless for the resolution of human problems without being coupled with forgiveness. Thus, one must be careful in treating love too romantically, since it is in itself far from a solution to human problems but rather is often what exacerbates human oppositions.

> "The blow of his Hammer is Justice, the
> swing of his Hammer Mercy,

The force of Los's Hammer is eternal
Forgiveness..."

Jerusalem, p.734

Note the contrast again. It is not a sweet, soft mercy nor a sweeping non-discriminating forgiveness which interests Blake but the contrast of "blow" and "force". There is power here, not weakness, and it may well be that it takes power, restrained power of course, to forgive, to grant mercy. The weak often have not the resilience and self-release for a generosity of spirit. And justice comes along with mercy. It is not as if mercy and forgiveness can suddenly make all things right. Actually, only a real sense of what injustices have been done can then move on with compassion.

(27.) Miracles

"As to Myself... I live by Miracle."

The Letters, p.795

Theologically, 'miracle' is given an exhalted place, but also usually a lonely place, one rare in its occurrence and next to impossible to understand. Instead, Blake places miracle in the middle of the substance of his daily life. Of course, he does not quite see this in the form of, say, Mary's immaculate conception, but he might see it as a little closer to Jesus' resurrection from the dead. Why? Because Blake's stress on imagination as the key to creativity makes the continuance of our life a daily resurrection from the dead, life born again where dullness might prevail, save for imagination.

(28.) Particularization

To Generalize is to be an Idiot.
To particularize is Alone the Distinction of Merit.
General Knowledges are those Knowledges that
Idiots possess.

Annotations to Reynolds, p.451

To generalize is too often to be an Idiot. Kierkegaard stressed the Individual against Hegel's vaunting of the Universal. Should Blake and Kierkegaard be right, we would have to rethink our enthusiasm for the Social Sciences. For only if human beings can be universalized, like the definition of water, do we possess the power to change social structures and individuals, as Hegel and Mao and others have proposed that we can do. Yet if the distinction of merit lies only in the particular, Marx's postulation of class struggle as a war between universal classes cannot hold firm. We must look for individual leaders in every field, all generalizations aside.

> What is General Nature? is there such a
> Thing? what is General Knowledge? is there such a
> Thing? Strictly Speaking all Knowledge is
> Particular.
>
> *Ibid.* p.459

Perfect forms, Blake tells us, are in the poet's mind, but they are there not from Nature but from Imagination. Plato knew real Forms, but they too were discovered by the power of Imagination, not taken from Nature or from sense experience. Thus, we must stop looking for general knowledge, except where chemicals and stars are concerned. If knowledge is particular, we must be careful about inventing universal ideas for man or woman which do not exist in fact. We should not give up what our imagination postulates, but we should be aware that all power lies in the individual, not in the universal.

(29.) Passion

> "If Sun & Moon should doubt,
> They'd immediately Go out.
> To be in a Passion you Good may do,
> But no Good if a Passion is in you."
>
> Ibid.,p.433

Where accomplishment is concerned, Blake sees passion as a two edged sword. But like Plato, he finds it necessary to achieve inspiration. Yet if passion turns and dominates you, it can thwart all constructive effort. Nevertheless, it is the only power which can form commitment and prevent doubt. Reason does not have that ability but rather seems to obstruct us when it does not have the flame of passion behind it.

(30.) Perception

> "If the doors of perception were cleansed, everything
>   would appear to man as it is, infinite.
> For man has closed himself up, til he sees all
>   things thro' narrow chinks of his cavern."
>   *The Marriage of Heaven and Hell*, p.154

At this point Blake almost joins the Rationalists. True, as all Moderns advised, our perception does need improvement. But there the comparison stops, since Blake offers it as no cure for our narrow vision. Unlike Spinoza, he does not suggest that we can all come to see as Gods do. Thus, the narrow perspective of our vision can be cured, but only by the imaginative individual. The majority cling to narrowness.

(31.) Philosophy

> "Hang Philosophy! I would not give a
> farthing for it! Do all by your feelings, and never
> think at all about it."
>   *An Island in the Moon*, p.51

This outburst cannot be taken literally, since Blake is himself a 'philosopher' by all classical meanings of that term. But this does show his love of decision and his realization that too much thought cuts out action and makes Hamlets of us all. He probably does not mean that we should not give thought prior to our actions, but he certainly does mean to say that, at some point, we must be prepared to let emotion commit us. Thought does not of itself lead to conclusion. We can only intuit the right time to bring philosophical examination to a halt and get on with life.

"Abstract Philosophy warring in enmity against Imagination.
(Which is the Divine Body of the Lord Jesus, blessed
forever...)"

Jerusalem, p.624

Having confronted reason with emotion and thought with
action, Blake now makes Imagination a force which must not let itself
be limited-- or perhaps we should say that novelty is in fact born in
oppositions. He also makes imagination to be the divine body of Jesus
Christ, and so it is clear that God's incarnation comes primarily as a
creative force, pressing to let reason go free and imagination to thrive.

"And Earth & all you behold;
        tho' it appears Without,
        it is Within,
In your Imagination, of which
        this World of Mortality is but
        a Shadow.

Jerusalem, p.709

Plato made the physical world a shadow to the world of
eternal Forms. Blake takes the inner world of the mind and makes the
outer world an image of that. We are not to take the physical world as
any less real than it appears. But we must never forget that without
God's creative and imaginative power, no natural order would or could
have descended. The divine imagination always comes first; without
that nothing is born by evolution. Thus, imagination frees us from the
confines of the physical world. As God does, we need to learn to
project the outer from the inner world by means of imagination.

(32.) Pity

Terror in the house does roar,
But Pity stands before the door.

Poems from the Notebook, 1800-3, p.421

Few comments of Blake could seem more contemporary, since we face terror all around us every day, not Utopias. It also contrasts to recent sentimental pictures of a Jesus who seems to offer pity out of weakness. The power of the Trinitarian doctrine is that it takes Jesus' full divinity seriously, in other words his sharing in the full majesty of divine power. Only if Jesus has-- whether apparent or hidden-- the full power of God does his forgiveness of sins have any meaning. Another weak person just like ourselves does not have enough authority to give wide forgiveness. But to wait, to stand quietly, need not represent weakness, since Jesus represents divine silence before Pilot.

> "And cans't thou die that I may live?
> "And cans't thou Pity & forgive?"
> *The Everlasting Gospel*, p.755

To pity and to forgive cannot be taken as the easy way out. They need a trade-off. Blake uses the classical notion sacrificing for another, even unto death. That is the real test of understanding and commitment. Pity and forgiveness that are effective in the world require this connection to power. But to learn this is perhaps the greatest gap in the Social Scientist's program. It may be that, in our teaching, we should stress that only power can balance contradictions. It cannot be done simply by rational resolution.

(33.) Religion

> Prisons are built with stones of Law,
>   Brothels with bricks of Religion.
> *The Marriage of Heaven and Hell*, p.151

This is true in the same way that Blake calls "the nakedness of women" the work of God. So that if religion with a puritanical bent restricts us from access, whether mentally or physically, then the mind and the body must find other avenues for satisfaction. Blake is right, in the lesser sense too, that most religions seem restrictive on the inventiveness of the human imagination. To preserve their hold on the follower, they think they must try to limit imaginative reconstruction. This is ironic, since all new religious insight comes from imagination's release from old doctrines. Thus, Blake cannot be "very religious", if that means to restrict new thought.

(34.) Salvation

> "O when shall the morning of the grave
> appear, and when
> Shall our salvation come? we sleep upon our watch,
> We cannot awake, and our Spectres rage
> in the forests.
> O God of Albion, where art thou?
> pity the watchers!"
>
> *Jerusalem*, p.671

Most religious notions of salvation stress the joy of release, assuming that this has already been accomplished. In a note perhaps more realistic, Blake stresses the agony of waiting for a promised fulfillment. "When?" is his question, not the usual joy of (pretended?) accomplishment. It is a mood which better fits the general agony in the world as the 21st century opens for us and the delay of, and our wish for, salvation is cast forward again.

(35.) Sensation

> By experiments of sense we become acquainted
> with lower faculties of the soul.
> Reason considers and judges of the imaginations.
>
> *Annotations to Berkeley*, p.774

Rather than bringing us all into a common understanding, empiricism unites us only by the lower faculties, not the higher. We can ascend from experiments of sense and "arrive at the highest". Yet this is not a democratic process but rather is an inspired, individual effort. The aim is not to move us toward some common understanding, but to allow the venturesome few some glimpse beyond that veil. The Modern Age thought that they had already, or would soon, lift the veil completely. However, with truth non-obvious and inspiration as our key, such a goal proves to be unfulfillable.

(36.) Sorrow

> "for sorrow is the lot of all of
> women born."
>
> *Poetical Sketches*, p.39

In addition to the benefit of unrestricted wandering, sorrow is traditionally seen by poets as a source of imagination, else what we are given is passively accepted. Sorrow is a natural state, and all who do not grasp this do not understand the human situation.

> "Excess of sorrow laughs. Excess of joy weeps."
>
> *Ibid.*, p.151

But sorrow can turn to comedy and joy to tears. We should not see either as far apart.

> "Joys impregnate. Sorrows bring forth."
>
> *Ibid.*

Nothing is born of the imagination except by contrast and by pain.

(37.) Soul/Thought

> "This world is Thine in which Thou
> dwellest; that within thy soul,
> That dark & dismal infinite where
> Thought roams up and down..."
>
> *Vala or the Four Zoas*, p.268

Blake reverses the intellectual's image of thought as ruling the soul or self. Plato leaves reason in control thus imposing strict order. But Blake sees the soul as in limitless space, a dark and dismal infinite, rather than the Light we associate with Plato's Forms. This fact incites thought to roam. The lostness of thoughts within the soul is, for him, not necessarily a negative image. Thought needs release from restriction if it is to become creative. The soul's vastness is disorienting, true; but it can also be novel-producing for the few. The worlds of the mind outnumber the Natural worlds, the naturally created orders, by far.

(38.) Truth

> A Truth that's told with bad intent
> Beats all the Lies you can invent.
>
> *Ibid.*, p.432

We hoped that truth might prove to be simple and simply out there for all of our ilk to observe whenever presented. But if, as Blake suggests, the intent of the presenter of truth is more important than detecting lies, then apprehending truth is always subject to distortion by its presenters. When complicated by human motives, truth seldom stands out pure and simple. So we must fathom the depths of the human heart before we can disentangle truth from it. Temperature can be read in numbers from a thermometer, but the truth which reveals the secrets behind the world's face is inaccessible to empiricists; it lies involved with the deep mysteries of the soul.

(39.) Try

> "Only Believe! Believe and try!
> Try, Try, & never mind the Reason why.
>
> *Epigrams, Verses, & Fragments,* p.536

Again, the mood is not one neither of reflection nor of dialectical discourse but is focused on the determination of the will. Blake holds out no promises of certain victory. The world is much too uncertain, human flesh too weak, to warrant romantic optimism. We commit first; belief does not come second. And our belief supports our attempts, not our certainty allowing our belief. Our test is whether we do not give up, not whether we have solved the human riddle. We express our puzzlement over the reality of the human dilemma. Yet unsolved mysteries can bring you to a stop. Or on the contrary they

can, once the new situation is accepted, promote you to try, try--
without ceasing.

(40.) Tyger

> Tyger! Tyger! burning bright
> In the forest of the night,
> What immortal hand or eye
> Could frame Thy fearful symmetry?
> Did he smile his work to see?
> Did he who made the Lamb make Thee?
>
> *Songs of Experience*, p.214

If anyone knows but one line of Blake, it is likely to be this
one about the Tyger. Although some may miss the poetic beauty of his
expression, Blake of course is linking God with terror and destruction,
as well as with creative artistry. God is the source of fearful symmetry
and so alone possesses the power to link these in Nature's creation.
Under less powerful guidance, they would split apart. Then no creation
would take place, only degeneration-- as our newspapers report every
day. Creative power, then, links beauty and terror, and so they must
be understood (or at least addressed) in combination.

(41.) Wisdom

> The Errors of the Wise Man make your Rule
> Rather than the Perfections of a Fool.
>
> *Epigrams, Verses*, p.550

Truth, as we now know, can never be simple or singular or
finished or complete, in spite of both Modern and Ancient dreams to
achieve rest and finality. Contemplation comes not from God, as
Aristotle wrongly thought, since the very structure of creation lies in
its constant contention. Aristotle thought the frame of the world
eternal, so that he could not conceive of its tortuous and terror-filled
evolutionary origins as Darwin did. Thus, the fool makes simple
statements and hopes for them to become universal and finished
truths, as Wittgenstein did when he excluded the mystical as being

outside 'truth'. The wise man knows the necessity to venture and so he or she will make mistakes. Yet this path lies closer to uncertain truths.

(42.) Youth

> Let age & sickness silent rob
> The vineyards in the night;
> But those who burn with vig'rous youth
> Pluck fruits before the light.
>
> *Poems from the Notebook, 1793*, p.172

Every decision doesn't have to be made now. The trick is to fix the right time and then to move before it is too late.

Blake again reverses tradition, this time about the convention that age brings wisdom. Truth being hidden as it is and also linked with terror, the vigorous, even the heedless youth is oddly better equipped for that dangerous venture. Truth cannot be sought in safety nor glimpsed without a struggle. So the aged, that is those who have given up the fight, are closed out. The venturesome, impulsive youth may be closer to truth's path, unless he or she thinks its capture yields rest. Where imagination and vigor abound, heedless of the dangers involved in truth's pursuit the necessary right approach is in fact close at hand.

II. THE METAPHYSICAL ASSUMPTIONS OF THE MODERN WORLD

Centuries ago Aristotle told us that most people, philosophers included, do not examine and criticize their basic principles. Instead, they assume them and simply argue from them. This does not mean that the assumptions of all ages and peoples are the same, nor does it require us to accept some theory of ultimate progress or of dialectical development. There can be new theories under the sun, in spite of any statement to the contrary. In fact, one of the virtues of the Modern Era was the confidence that they had broken out of ancient and inhibiting assumptions and so we're coming close to controlling their own destiny in order to improve the lot of the entire human species.

As the 20th Century turns toward a new one, the assumptions of the Modern World stand out more clearly to us than they could have to the founders of that Era. Just as their age advanced by questioning long held Ancient and Medieval assumptions, so the 21st century must now break new ground by distinguishing itself from its Modern predecessors. "Post-Modern" has recently become a catch phrase. It tends to offer us a rather esoteric mode of thought, one not widely accessible and one possibly still tied to its century of origin. In this essay we will take Blake's remarks on creativity and use the poet's approach to intellectual advance to try to highlight the assumptions of the Modern Age which must be critiqued if we are to survive and move into a New Century armed with new creativity.

A. The Rationalists: Descartes, Leibniz and Spinoza

(1.) All who study Descartes recognize the importance of his idea of God. He assumes that his notion of divinity is universally shared, at lest by all rational people. It offers him the needed prime example of the clear and distinct ideas which Descartes sought in order to establish a criteria for certainty in human knowledge. The Medieval world had, on the whole, placed God outside the possibility of final human comprehension. But to accomplish his goal, Descartes must banish all transcendence and thus any trace of mysticism. That is, he must do so if he is to achieve certainty, which he wanted to do by copying what he thought was the about-to-be- achieved certainty of scientific and mathematical knowledge.

The problem with his idea of God, Aristotle would want us to point out, is that it assumes its key concept of God rather than arguing to the truth of it. Thus, if God is not like Descartes' description, the king pin of his theory falls. Of course, Descartes was simply bringing his conception of God into line with the scientific advance in his time. Thus, after centuries of uncertainty and struggle over the nature of God, he thought divinity too needed to be tamed and brought within human control. The irony is that, just as Darwin's evolutionary theory upset theological orthodoxy, Darwin's evolutionary God does not fit Descartes' theory of clear and distinct ideas. Divinity's selection of such a long, destructive, and wasteful evolutionary path to creation does not argue for a God of clarity and reason but rather for one who can move through dark avenues to novelty.

Could Descartes prove to us his assumptions about the nature of God, which are so crucial to his project and yet which now appear to be so questionable for the 21st century? His argument was circular. God would be such as he described, that is, if divinity were a Rationalist. Also the Rationalist's project needs God to be as Descartes described divinity in order not to cast the whole program of knowledge into doubt. Could God have the emotions of Yahweh; or could divinity be the cause of fear and trembling, as Kierkegaard said was true of his deity; or should God even opt for Darwin's painful and tortuous path to create humanity, then human knowledge could neither be a simple thing nor could God's intentions be made fully and rationally plain.[2]

Of course, part of Descartes' uncriticised assumptions come from the "wallpaper on the walls of the age", i.e., they assumed the arrival of Progress over the past and the coming completion of knowledge. No later criticism of Descartes or the Rationalists needs to deny the accomplishment of that age. The issue is: Do the mathematics and the scientific advances which they saw arriving really foreshadow an extension of rational knowledge to include the control of human nature, thus enabling us to reach beyond our former bounds? The Social Sciences were born of the assumption that man could be studied just like the stars or a mathematical axiom. That is a startling advance--if it is true. But as the 21st century dawns, the Chaos and Complexity we find present does not give us any evidence, or even hope, that we have in fact advanced beyond the constant threat of a return to our primitive origins.

(2.) Leibniz is perhaps most popularly known for his version of the theory of the "best of all possible worlds." Ironically however, it is the advance of science, particularly medicine, which calls into question his assumptions about God as the ultimate Rationalist creator. Our medical advance, not to mention our walking on the moon, proves that knowledge has come into existence which could greatly improve the human lot. Cancer, Aids, small pox, surgery, anesthesiology and anesthetics-- all these prove that the long centuries of unrelieved pain and the shortness of life do not now need to be as before. A non-Modern-Rationalist God could have decided to conceal these secrets about our natural ability to overcome defects and so doom men and women to centuries of removable pain, but a divinity for century-twenty-one certainly could not be a God governed by Leibnez's happy principles.

Leibniz also has his theory of Monads, one in which our lives are open to our own interior perception as programmed in advance from eternity. But his is a God who denies freedom of the will to man in order to keep the divine perception clear and complete. Leibniz does not question his assumptions of the fixity of knowledge or of a

---

[2] c.f., Damasio, Antonia R. Descartes' Error. Avon Books, New York, 1995.

divinity who fixes our future. Whereas, if God prized freedom as the chief divine attribute, he should be willing to accept uncertainty into the divine understanding thus restricting omniscience. Then, it could be that we are not a Monad, locked within ourselves simply working to clarify our perception of a fixed nature, but are in fact free and contingent beings -- not at all unlike God.

(3.)   It is easy to see that, in the Modern Era, imagination plays little part in the search for truth. There is no need for it; truth lives in front of us (Empiricism) or inside of our minds (Rationalism), and so we need universal conformity in philosophy in order to match our knowledge with the expected universal theory emerging in all of science. Spinoza is sure that we can come to think as God does. He equates the substance of the natural world with God's substance, now extended to infinity. That is, we can achieve a divine mode of knowledge, if our thought becomes steady and free of emotion, as God's is. We can imagine how God thinks, but when we do so we see that emotion (that driving force behind all imagination) should be, will be, eliminated as we become more fully rational, just as Spinoza assumes that God is and always has been, emotion being simply a product of our not seeing all "under the aspect of eternity."

"Freedom," of course, simply comes to mean to understand the necessary origin of our ideas and all of our actions. Mind and body are equated in any true understanding. This eliminates the traditional notion that, however obvious our physical bodies and the natural universe might become, the soul of man remains illusive and inevitably subject to fault and corruption, no matter how perfect our mastery of numbers might be. Descartes has trouble finding a connection between mind and body in order to allow their interaction; Spinoza postulates their parallelism, in spite of the fact that their disparity is the main source of human problems. The issue is: Can this disparity, would it, was it, could it be overcome in the Modern Era?

Spinoza's God is, of course, fully rational, and in divinity, knowledge is complete. Only we incomplete humans are still unknowing about the source and control of emotion. But improving our understanding can eliminate emotion, a rather necessary premise for Continental Rationalism. But this is an assumption totally at odds with our own experience of the continued desparity between our own fallible reason and our too often uncontrolled emotions. We can assume, as Spinoza does, that what has been true throughout our history will now cease to be so as our Enlightenment spreads. But of course, like Descartes, again this all depends on whether God is in fact fully dominated by reason as Spinoza postulates divinity to be.

Could God, as is true of human nature, be as much fascinated by freedom (in the sense of indeterminacy) as we are? How could it be that the divinity who stands at the origin of the universe should have a nature so different from the creatures who evolved? What would lead us to believe, given our still escalating violent history, that we will no longer be racked by devastating emotions or that a divinity would create us so that, either at the beginning or at some point in our evolution, emotion and indeterminism would cease to be a governing human principle? Spinoza has in fact simply constructed a God, not from our evolving human experience, but from a non-natural notion of the completion of reason and the elimination of disturbing emotion. Now, as the 21st century approaches, we are forced to challenge that premise, just as Aristotle recommends.

B. The Elimination of Metaphysics

For Aristotle "metaphysics" meant the comparative study of all of the available first principles. This becomes the prime reflective-critical business of all philosophers, vs. the majority who simply assume their principles and proceed. If so, why was it a constant diatribe and theme of the Modern Era to eliminate metaphysics? Because they had to assume, in order to make the "Modern Dream" come true, that there was not a plurality of first principles or postulates, any one of which we might assume and argue for, but instead that there was, finally, a growing singular theoretical first principle which all true philosophers could unite upon and accept. Hume's mitigated skepticism and Wittgenstein's refusal to give up the-mystical-beyond were two exceptions to this trend, as well as Pascale's Candide.

Thus, all philosophers are required to begin by making a choice between the first principles available to them. We must argue for the first principles we select, while at that same time admitting that other philosophers could begin from different premises and still be true philosophers. Must one assume the Modern starting point as his or her necessary first principle, or is the world and philosophy itself plural by nature, however much such a fact defeats all finality in theory? Of course, the physical sciences at one time saw themselves headed toward unity and finality. Odd, isn't it, that as science has retreated from the goal of completion, many philosophers still cling to it as their inherited dream.

In the 21st century, will metaphysics again become "first philosophy", as Aristotle originally named it? If we do not have an agreed starting point in method for all sciences and all philosophy, to which each of its practitioners must agree, we have no choice but to begin philosophy over again in each new day, comparing and evaluating all the first principles from which we might start. Imagination, then, is not simply an interference to be eliminated, as much of the Modern World thought. Rather, it is a necessity; we need it to inspire the mind to new concepts, since we can no longer take for granted the finality of the Modern starting point. Certainly theoretical physics and mathematics are today the major inspirers of imaginative thought, rather than of fixity and finality as the Moderns postulated would become true. Thus, philosophy can no longer eliminate metaphysics or assume any one starting point. Instead, it is assigned to an uncertainty in all of its principles.

Has there, then, been no progress since the Middle Ages, which was disparaged because of its obscurity and lack of progress? Certainly, there has been. St. Thomas could not conceive of man walking on the moon or of God embracing uncertainty or of any divinity using waste and terror as founding principles. The whole medieval theological design was too rational, too fixed, too secure; the tortuous waste of evolution would be offensive to their theological vision. But our anticipated progress has proved continually flawed. It has been one sided and physical. Many had hoped to leave the spiritual behind, just because of its illusive quality. But if the physical world's exploration does not lead to such finality and to cumulative progress, as we so long supposed, perhaps the spiritual is in fact central to our ability to deal constructively with our continued problems. Then, it is not our physical nature or even the cosmos that is the origin of our continued faults, particularly if these two worlds were not created to be parallel, as Spinoza postulated.

C. The Empirical Hope

If we hoped to find certainty and a universally agreed point of theoretical reference, then of course the natural world confronting and opening up to us might be assumed to be our best hope for a stable point of reference. But what if Reason and the human Mind are not as obvious as we had hoped they would become? Freud, of course, shows himself as the ultimate Rationalist, since he thinks that the murky depths of the soul can be rendered fully rational. Of course, he is psychologically based vs. Spinoza's divine obsession. But our experience since Freud's time has shown us that there is no final agreement about the causes and the origins of our spiritual problems today, not even if we banish all religions. Freud hoped for a unity of theory, thus his near rage at Jung's theoretical defection, because the depths of the mind should no longer puzzle us. But Jung began to see mystical uncertainty as an inevitable fact. Nevertheless, if Modern psychology fails in its founding goals, how about our grasp of physical nature?

Sense perception seems at first to be a common human denominator, a perhaps preferable point of unity for agreed reference. Could the Empiricists have achieved unity of all behind their doctrine, just as Freud hoped that all psychiatrists would unite with him, perhaps Empiricism might have been our best hope to achieve agreement in our starting point for truth. But in fact the Empiricists diverged from the beginning, e.g. Locke and Berkeley not to mention Hume and Hobbes. Thus, Empiricism today is not only not unified but cannot be universally accepted as philosophy's starting point. Moreover, as a doctrine it is unable to meet all our needs, since the human soul seems only slightly empirically oriented. In fact, imagination can hardly be held within any empirical bounds, which is both its virtue and its vice and also why it is often so difficult to bring to fruition. But if they were so desirable because of their consequences, why were Locke's first principles not obvious and universally accepted?

1.) Locke's God and the Empirical Order

Locke envisions a God, a rather quiet and sedate divinity, who might use sense experience, rather than spiritual experience, as a creating principle. However, Locke's 'primary substance,' which he hoped would offer a universal standard, does not conform to his 'secondary substance', which begins to involve more subjectivity and individuality. Thus, 'experience,' that is, sense experience, is not quite so universal a standard of reference as one might have hoped. Furthermore, it is obvious that its acceptance as our agreed reference also assumes some universal standard of education. Locke does not begin with the natives of the South Pacific or with the Zulus of South Africa. There is nothing wrong, of course, with setting a goal of universal education. It is just that, even in England, it does not apply to all classes, and when considered world-wide it hardly exists at all as an accepted human touchstone.

If our experience is not standardized by nature but instead depends on the hope of imposing a common education , then the empirical world, which does lie in front of us all, is not so helpful as we might suppose, in spite of the fact of being universally available. What we bring to it from the depths of our souls proves much more important and hardly subject to standardization. So perhaps God is not an empiricist after all. Instead, in the instant of the launching an evolving creation, divinity decided to use a much more diverse and non-standard organizing principle. It was one more emotionally centered than focused on sense experience, thus making imagination more crucial than external observation in our search for truth.

2.) Hobbes and the State of Nature

Hobbes knew that we had not begun in the way that a culturally oriented educational system has finally rendered at least some of us to perform as citizens. But he seemed sure that, by accepting a system of government, we could contain any tendency of ours to return to our more primitive and destructive state. However, if by nature we begin less rationally controlled and are in fact still naturally aggressive, what could restrain us from returning to the "state of nature," which seems to happen so frequently today? Even Hobbes, with his less charitable assessment of our basic human nature, assumes that government and education will prevail, that all will seek and accept this controlling role and thus agree to unite under a domesticating rule. But he seems to have underestimated our constant pull toward anarchy.

Even if our origins render us less universally domesticatable then either the Rationalists or Locke might have hoped, and if we have not truly left primitiveness behind, there might still be some chance to develop a standard form of philosophical reference by using an agreed first principle, a common philosophical starting point or system or methodology. But if every time the political state does not meet our particular purposes we tend to reject accepted social structures and retreat to more primitive forms of aggression, then any agreed social framework will not hold except perhaps momentarily. If our native aggressions always lies just below any domesticated surface, no acquired social system or philosophical methodology can produce an accepted universal reference, since our native power drives, as Darwin stressed so much, remain still primary.

3.) Berkeley and God again.

Much as both the Rationalists and the Empirical traditions hoped to get away from the God-oriented Middle Ages, for all of them divinity appears again and again as the calming standard of universal reference. On the surface of our experience "Reason" is hardly one thing for us all, and so for centuries we tried to use sense experience. But we have not found it a universalizing standard that brings agreement to philosophy. Oddly, then, God must serve as a simple and agreed standard of reverence for both Rationalism and Empiricism else they may find none. Yet even more oddly, looking at the variety of images of the divine which exist world-wide, hardly anything could be further from the case than that all religious traditions, even all Western concepts, will ever agree about the nature of divinity. Our many Gods have different natures, not simply different names which we give to a supposed unity, helpful as such a single divinity might have been could we discover one.

Thus, much as they hoped to escape the God-centrality of the Middle Ages, if God is not found to be a single rational, standard concept among all men and women, the hoped for unity in Empiricism and in Rationalism is threatened. Berkeley, of course, has God hold his empirical world in continued existence, because he is aware that the world as we experience it is far from a steady. But if Berkeley needs God to hold our sense experience in existence, then it is not our normal sensory experience which provides us with our universal standard but only our acceptance of some one notion of God. If that is to be our basis for agreement then as every day goes by it seems less likely to hold--as we speed destructively into the New Century.

4.) Hume and the Necessity of Empirical Skepticism

Hume's skepticism is one of the few agreements to come out of the Modern Age. That is, sense experience does not at all provide as much universalizable certainty as we had hoped. Instead, it leads at best to a mitigated skepticism, that is as far as obtaining universal agreement is concerned. If so, we are still searching for the standard of philosophy that will equal the once expected universality of the sciences. The physical sciences had seemed to offer universality and certainty. But when philosophers attempted to use either Reason or Sense Experience as their norm, no such universality and necessity emerged.

All the while, the physical sciences have been moving further and further away from sense experience, and also from any single and final theory. Thus, neither mathematics nor physics achieved the theoretical universality and finality which philosophy hoped it could imitate. As the century closes, Hume's skepticism about the bed-rock finality of sense experience is in fact mirrored by the increasing diversity in scientific theory. Hume also gives a wider birth to emotion in human decisions, and the speculative scientist knows that inspiration is more important to theoretical advance then had once been hoped (due to our emotions often uncontrollable and even destructive nature.) Have we then retreated back to the Middle Ages, or even to Ancient times? Not at all. We have progressed, but only as accompanied by an ultimate plurality and the continued uncertainty of truth. Our amazing advance in learning has led us to a "learned ignorance," as Nicholas Cusanus foresaw. We learn; we accomplish much with our science; but our added insights only allow us to see more of what we could not and did not know in our innocence that still remains unknown. Our increased knowledge has increased our awareness of all that we did not know and perhaps can never know with finality.

D. Are All the Modern Advances Negated?

Certainly not. But the Modern world did not, and we now realize could not, achieve its hoped for finality. We learned to walk on the moon, true enough. We control an atomic power unknown to any ancient tribe, but the hope once and for all to leave our ancient condition behind has proved impossible. If we take Darwin as our model for "The Age to Come", rather than the Empiricists or the Rationalists, we know that Darwin traces no linear line of progress. Instead, he grants us some ability to control our own destiny; once we reach an "Age of Reason" our advance is possible. He does not condemn us to stay in a primitive state forever. But he knows how close we always are to our origins and how fiercely we are still locked into a primitive struggle for survival . Like our personal computers, our celebrated achievements may crash at any time, especially without constant vigilance.

But if even the physical sciences cannot come to a final unity and agreement and closure on theory but instead remain constantly open to innovation, certainly philosophy can expect no less for itself. We are back to Plato's conviction that truth cannot be stated with finality in any systematic or verbal form, and also Aristotle's belief that our first principles are not given to us in unity and finality but rather must constantly be appraised against one another. That is possible and some certainty is achievable, but it sustains itself only in certain restricted areas. The Modern Age thought that the metaphysical comparison of first principles had become unnecessary due to scientific advance. But if we have returned to plurality and a continued uncertainty in theory, metaphysics again becomes "first philosophy," as Aristotle called it, since we are still locked into an irreducible plurality of basic concepts. They are rich stimulators of the human imagination, but their plurality also blocks us from gaining the peace and rest that we thought finality and certainty would bring.

III. DISCOVERING TRUTH, APPRAISING TRUTH

But wait; from our common philosophical tradition you rightly remind us that we are not only to seek the truth but also to try to establish standards for its assessment. Plato has the Forms, difficult as they are to fit into final expression, and Aristotle developed a tighter system of categories for philosophical verification. Each philosopher and each age can be characterized by its criteria for establishing truth. If the Modern Age, which hoped for completion and unity and finality in theory, has proved wrong in its basic assumptions, that is that they were not so clearly the obvious starting points as they had hoped, then is all verification to be abandoned to individual instinct?

Not at all. The ancient task of the comparison of first principles returns, not flooding us with a radical relativism as our 20th century tended sometimes to assume. Ours is simply a task that knows no end, where again and again the questions become more important than finalized answers, where the future remains open not closed, and where human freedom returns as an option even at the expense of constant uncertainty. One can hold a position. All theories are not equally fruitful, as every physical scientist admits. But it is up to us to establish criteria, while admitting that our now preferred theories, in spite of their advantages, cannot be the single starting point for all, or even possibly not for very many, as an uncertain future unfolds. The diversity of cultures involves the diversity of philosophical/theological principles, but all are not therefore equally valuable-- neither every culture nor every theory.

The Empirical tradition sought truth in "experience." The Pragmatists sought to verify truth by practical consequences. Both are right, but with two important qualifications: (1) "Experience" is not in fact some uniform and obvious matter; rather it is closer to the classic notions of 'Being,' i.e., a general term referring to everything possible in existence. Our human 'Experience' now stands for everything that is, since all the possible structures of every world now fall under our observation, either directly or by technological advance. But our experience, our very being, is not singular and uniform. It is rather multifaceted and diverse, as all life before us tends and will tend to be. All standards are not gone; all cultures and philosophies are not equal; reason still has its task of appraisal, which is all the more difficult and important now just because the Modern hope for an ultimate simplicity in theory has not been realized.

Therefore, our job as philosophers becomes more important, not less so due to the advancement of science, as it would not have been true had Empiricist or Rationalist assumptions proved to hold firm. The physical sciences not only do not offer us a final standard for truth but instead simply add complexity to former truth. William Blake and the power of imagination now enter in force. For if there is no final standard but rather many truths (not falsities but truths), then our primary question becomes: What can lead us to new perceptions and insights, since neither the facts simply before us nor the impressions in our present experience are not sufficient to determine truth's future forms. The theoretical physicist has imagination; he or she must have in order to advance. So passion and imagination return to lead philosophical research, a new form of necessity. Perhaps they are our only real necessity now.

1.) Pragmatism Extended
        In American Pragmatism, which has a certain similarity to Existentialism in wanting to use each individual's life experience to form our standard, the assumption was that an immediate practical test might validate the truth we wished to establish. But except for certain obvious physical experiments which hardly exist in life or in scientific

investigation, we often have to wait some length of time, perhaps years, before the future tells us which assumption   proved finally fruitful.   So Pragmatism must extend its time line, immediate confirmation being hardly possible on any question of significance. As a matter of fact, we seldom expect any instant confirmations.

We want to know, whether in theoretical science or in our individual lives, what really works vs. theory postulated-- Pragmatism is right. But our time line needs to be pushed forward. Further, such results are often rather particular not universal, at least for human individuals if not in science. In that case, early Pragmatism assumed the possibility of a universality of results which we must now doubt. If the physical sciences to do not need to account for individuality, we must do so in our human life or distrust all truth. Universality holds only superficially in human nature.   This makes our use of the Pragmatic test of practical results crucial, but unfortunately it seldom extends neatly from one person to another. Thus, we both must wait, sometimes long intervals for human test results, but even then these often cannot be extended beyond the individual.

2.) Existentialism Revisited

Sartre, as we know, gave up God, in spite of the importance of the concept of divinity in our lives and in his theory, because he thought that the traditional God's fixity of knowledge denied human freedom.   Thus, Sartre focused on Kierkegaard's weakness: the traditional God vs. radical human freedom.   Kierkegaard had been aware of the paradox of human uncertainty vs. God's certainty, but Sartre moved to eliminate God in order to protect human freedom and self-determination. Yet if we are fully free, or if at least we could be if we became decisive, then the function of God which all the Moderns assumed, that is to be a point of reference and stability, is eliminated. Our decisiveness becomes our own not God's and cannot be predicted, although God usually has a better grasp on the possibilities and the odds than we do. Las Vegas is an example to divine uncertainty, but as the divine T.V. monitors show all the horse races being run simultaneously, it is coupled with a knowledge of the odds that favor the house.

If this is the case, "truth" cannot be uniformly predicted where we humans are concerned, although some of us are lucky.

Thus, the hope for a universal reference for truth is frustrated on the human side, all the while physical truth became more diverse and complex and uncertain than we once hoped. There is a certain sense in which human contingencies has turned and invaded the physical sciences, rather than the sciences establishing universal norms of certainty which human sciences could then follow. We had hoped to bring human nature into line with physical certainty. Instead, the natural sciences find themselves facing some of the uncertainty which human beings have always faced, even though they have, like God, developed powerful tools for testing possibilities and options.

3.) God's Re-entry

There is a vast irony in fact that the Modern thinkers, almost to a man and woman, kept divinity as a central support for their certainty, all the while they moved toward theoretical completion using the model of the Natural Sciences. However, the uncertainty, chaos, complexity, and incompleteness of theory which overtook our scientific hopes for certainty and finality at first eliminated God, whether for Sartre or for Bertrand Russell. But then, as science becomes radicalized in its theory, coming closer to Existential thought in its non-finality, God is again allowed to serve as a focal point, but this time in the more traditional guise coupled with mysticism and transcendence. God need no longer be eliminated in order to establish a scientific certainty, since that hope has been passed by.

Of course, there is no necessity for the 21st century philosopher to use God as a focus for his or her theory, since uncertainty can again be established on human grounds alone without appealing to the mysticism which divinity's traditional dress involves. But neither the fixity of Modern theory nor the uncertainty of contemporary physics either excludes or includes God. Like all human decisions, God's inclusion is a free decision and can be determined individually. A free God, one who is individual in his or her decisions, can be the model for human individual determination. Theoretical certainty does not demand an omniscient God, however our constant human uncertainty at least allows the presence of God within any philosophical framework.

4.) Truth and Uncertainty in the 21st Century

The Modern world took uncertainty to be antithetical to the establishment of truth. They tailored their Gods to accomplish their purpose of finality. But as both the physical sciences and mathematics moved away from one fixed mode of truth, and as Existentialism made our lives less certain and more subject to individual determination, God and the physical sciences can--not must--merge once again. This time not because both require fixity, certainty, finalized knowledge and singularity of theory, but rather because each is now subject to the limits defined by a universe which exhibits various degrees of freedom and flexibility.

Are there thus no standards for truth? Certainly there are, just no single or fixed one. But all notions of progress are gone, if we mean by that a linear progress that outmodes all before it. True, the physical sciences become more sophisticated and complex, while human nature has not been finalized in theory, in spite of the hopes of Hegel and Marx and Freud. It is simply that we must stand ready to start over with our human nature every day and look for new and theoretically fruitful theories in science that appear due to individual imagination. The worlds we live in are multiple and many-faceted. And our mind lives in and explores many more than the obvious world in front of us, thank God. Pace Empiricists and Rationalists!

Postscript I

A. The Age of Exploration

Blake is the child of our time, not his. He was largely either misunderstood or ignored by his own Age. Perhaps this was because his venturesomeness and creativity went against Modern Times, that age so beautifully satirized by Charlie Chaplin. Blake pioneers; he recommends the exploration of the possible worlds within the mind, all the while his own time concentrated either on the actual empirical world or on socio-political structures. Why? Because Blake realized that the possible worlds, in which creative mind dwells, are in fact closer to the origins of all human understanding. Again, why? Because the exploration of our minds' various worlds which open to us is what spawns all human creativity--as well as its uncertainty and terror.

There was once an age of exploration which went out to the New World and then around the globe, and recently the exploration of space reached a climax when man walked on the moon. Now, it is inner space's turn to launch our voyages. Scientific exploration propelled philosophers into their empirical phase, even pushed them into trying to finalize a theoretical certainty. But now we know better than that, since this quest has led us into our present age which has too often stalemated for lack of imagination. 'Thought', they said, meant first to have empirical impressions and then to rearrange them so as to produce new ideas. Such cannot be the origin of creativity, most of us now believe; and Disney is certain of it. Then why bother with outer perceptions any longer, if the inner world is more expansive and in its vast extent lies still largely unexplored? Off we go, following physics and mathematics again-- where we find only minimum empirical attachment. We realize that all that we encounter in those sciences is as such not simply empirically true, but it can still move the mind's process by inspiration. Although our visible society is too often dull or unproductive, physics and mathematics seem to dwell more in inner worlds than in the outer, whatever empirical usefulness we may discover for them.

So we find ourselves propelled out into a New Age of Exploration. Hegel thought that we marched to the drum of a universal logic, one that mirrored the physical/social world's historical process. Such a philosophical key to the world's understanding seemed also to offer us a control over the future, or so the Marxists and the Utopians were sure. In that case that major Adventure seemed to lie in controlling/improving social/political structures. Next, as kings and dictators fell and human rights were proclaimed and democracies arose, who could doubt that creativity lay in exploring every new social concept? Next, Freud was certain that he could extend this into the mind's depths, even to its always unseen recesses. His project was also based on a strict Rationalism, believing that everything driving the soul could be rendered rational by the use of one universal technique. Biography was not really individual but rather a universal plot acted out on a uniform cultural scene. We could control all this thought if we could universalize and rationalize all of human nature-- and individual biography in the process.

As our century closes, we see that too much remains tied to unique behavior; there is too much that escapes any rational net; there are sources in the soul that lie beneath anyone's grasp, not even God's fully. Yet, the social and political worlds remain almost in the same state of uncontrol, subject to destruction or tyranny, just as they were yesterday. Thus, tomorrow's utopias seem further from our grasp than ever, even given the occasional bright spots that may appear. Creativity often opens up to us, not from the outer sense but from our inner sense, and on the occasion of its production it presents itself as radically individual rather than as universal. The signs along the highways of physical space, or among the forces that play on the social and political stage, may seem rather clear compared to the depths or the "black holes" of inner space we now explore.

Of course, we have always realized that our art, our literature, our music sprang more from the soul's inner depths then from any common outer sensations, however much what the eye and ear saw and heard might have served as material for our inspiration. All of us are not equally creative or innovative, and we should have been, had our imagination been a function of our outer sense and so dependent on our perception of the visible world. This is perhaps why the scientific age so much deprecated art and poetry and all that it could not see and render fully rational. But today philosophy, like all imaginative work whether in finance or in industry, seems to be more a product of inner, idiosyncratic vision than of any standardized act of perception.

Theology, too, suffered in the Modern Age, because it had so often dealt with things unseen. Nothing was to transcend the observable world, the Modern Utopian Prophets declared. Today our visible world seems to need transcending--that is, if its to be made livable. In order to create the Modern World, nothing was to exceed human grasp, as all mystics had agreed that God did. But nothing so much exceeds our control as that which makes God's appearance possible again in the 21st century, even if it comes more from chaos arising in the depths of the soul than from its heights. Our world-changing imagination appears to arise from those who are specially attuned. It seems to invade our minds like an immense force which merely touches us with only a slight brush-- just as many had reported about their brief encounter with the divine-- but evidencing an overpowering source. It is here that our explorations for the 21st century begin, blind guide that science has proved to be where our soul's health and balance are concerned.

B. Into the 21st Century: Out of Control?

The dream of the Modern Age was to achieve a perfect knowledge and to use this power to control the future, both natural and human. As that hope fades away into the sunset of the closing century, is our situation in fact now such that our only hope is to learn to offer a rapid response to change, to react quickly to chance factors, forces that may not ultimately lie in our control fully to direct? All change was to come under our direction, we Moderns thought. Now we see ourselves, not so much as about to tame all the spiritual and mental lions, but more as if we are being asked each day to take on the forces of change which threaten to swallow us if we are not quick enough, or adventuresome enough, in our responses. And this is not something we can all be trusted, or counted on, to do as educationally trained experts. Like the few super-athletes we admire, some of us are gifted with the ultimate quickness of response, which arises more from imagination than as the response to a power which any manual of instruction could instill.

Education, then, should not contrive to teach us old tricks, except as our teachers may show us how the inventions of the past, whether medical or physical or mathematical or artistic or theological, may have spurred the imagination of those who lived before us to move beyond their past and their present limitations. Hegel had hoped that our history, when understood dialectically, would lead us (or some powerful leaders) to control it and so to trace out the future.   But because the future does not arise from the simple inter-play of forces in our past but rather is subject to the surprising intervention of novelty and chance, history cannot bring chaos into strict prediction, and complexity is often too much for most standard minds (or computers) to master, no matter how conventionally brilliant we become.   'Education' comes to mean our imaginative response, however much it may rest on both standard accumulation of information and unconventional instinct.

Can we, need we, bring our schools back under our control so that they instill some discipline vs. the disorder which prevails so widely today in all education? Should we not try to eliminate violence on all levels of society by teaching the use of imagination? But this will only happen, of course, when our mind is well grounded in an ingrained basic discipline so as to enable any individual who is dedicated and willing to commit himself/herself to human advance. Everyone doing anything he or she wants to do at any time, learning to obey no order either from themselves or from others-- this is not, it cannot be, the avenue to our advance into the New Century. Creativity is lost in chaos, and imagination is stifled because the self, having adopted no discipline, cannot direct its own energies but can only let them run untamed.

Anarchy has always been associated with individualism in America's self image, but our resources are now too vulnerable, both physical and human to yield to that wild temptation. Thus, we must blend discipline with individualism, or else, we will stumble into the next century only to fall exhausted. Education, all education whether physical or spiritual or mental, must offer to instill a basic power of self control so that our individual talents can be self-directed, since there is no agreed universal formula. Our educational problem is not that there is a lack of talent in the young. Recent disasters in our schools are more due to a waste of human resources through our inability to control and to direct them productively. Should the reverse of this self-destruction not be the aim of all education in the New Century?

All the young must learn to obey, first those who attempt to teach them and then themselves. Few can develop an inner self-control unless they learn first to accept outer direction from another, however much easier and tempting it is not to believe that. But those who instruct the young must remember, and make it quite evident, that the aim of all discipline is to make self-control possible, not to induce conformity. It is impossible to conceive what our world would look like if every natural and latent talent in every individual had learned how to make itself productive, had acquired the self-control needed to obey itself and so to cease simply to rebel against others and themselves. To refuse to accept either our society or its tyrants in an oppressive and degenerative state--to rebel against such conditions as Camus advised us to do--that we should always try. But this can only be effective if our education has first equipped us with the inner discipline needed to exert self-control and thus to direct our energies effectively rather than simply to explode.

C. The Human Comedy Replayed

Philosophically, politically, religiously, we have too often lost the wider meaning of, and the human guidance provided by, comedy and humor. We often take 'comedy' to mean a happy ending, a Frank

Capra movie or Shakespeare's "All's Well that Ends Well." We have so long thought in utopian scripts that we cannot accept or reconcile the tragedies that are daily reported all around us with our ideal to transform human nature--or at least we do not let that enter into our optimistic views of the future. John Carey, the English literary critic, makes an important distinction for us which we need to keep in mind as we enter the 21st Century while leaving our Utopian dreams at the gate. "Tragedy is tender to man's dignity and self-importance, and preserves the image that he is a noble creature. Comedy uncovers the absurd truth, which is why people are so afraid of being laughed at in real life."[3]

Marxists Dictators, and sometimes too often priests and teachers, allow no laughter, see nothing comic in themselves, in us, or in their new-order proposals. Utopian schemes in themselves may not be funny but are often quite inspiring, just as Christianity or Buddhism or Marxism has been and still can be. Neil Simon's "Laughter on the 23rd floor" illustrates why he is a successful playwright: He can laugh at himself and at his fellow writers, all the while recognizing their creative talent and their seriousness about life. They are aware of our constant human foibles, whereas Marx thinks that these can be eliminated or at least will be repressed. Our problem in creating new ideal societies, new religions to save us, is that the people who lead us often take themselves too seriously and so block out the recognition of the absurd in us all. Marx thinks he can remove the absurdity, and thus the humor, from human nature. Instead, Camus would have us focus on absurdity, as the only way to understand the obscurity in human nature and to visualize our future.

This may be one reason why Existentialism has been popular in literary and artistic circles but has often been avoided by "serious philosophers." It highlights the absurdity and irrationalities in so many of our intellectual/political pretensions. One may not need a sense of humor in physics; but in sociology and politics and psychology it can be a fatal flaw to ignore or to lack a sense of the absurdity that prevails in "the human condition". We expect our leaders, whether political, religious, or social to lack flaws, and then we often ignore their repeated tragedies to our peril. We can achieve; we have wrought changes; but where men and women are concerned

---

[3] Carey, John. Here Comes Dickens. Schocken Books. New York, p.7

very little of this has been on a mass-produced basis. So if our projected plans for improvement, whether individual or social, depend for their success on our flawless universal execution (e.g. Marx), we are in for another disappointment in our "Great Expectations."

Carey reports: "Humanity's attempt to surround its puny concerns with gravity and decorum seemed to [Charles] Dickens hilarious."[4] Does this mean that we laugh during church prayers and at presidential inaugurations? No, these do not involve puny concerns. But in every case we tend too quickly to envelope each ceremony in the cloak of an impenetrable seriousness. T.V. "sitcoms" and country-western lyrics return us to reality, which is why they are so successful and why we also desperately need political cartoonists. There are frequent inconsistencies in Dickens's writing, Carey reports, an "error" which he feels is actually vital to the imaginative writer. We too often witness an attempt to cover up every inconsistency in politics and in society, rather than use this to induce laughter into our homes.

What is " really real"? Marx and Hegel thought that their theories circumscribed the Real, which is why 'deviation' from theory becomes a cardinal sin. One does not revise what is real and true, and that is why calling one a "revisionist" was not a term of praise but of abuse, a label often ending with facing the firing squad. "The power of imaginative literature [is] to refashion the reader's circumscribed notions about what constitutes the real..."[5] Plato, you remember, in his later writing revised his doctrine of the Forms and came to define the "real" as whatever has "power." This elevates many things and action and thoughts to the status of the "real" which have none of the classic characteristics of Plato's Forms, e.g., timelessness. This metaphysical change results in a less neat world for Plato, and therefore many who follow him have ignored the later, the more complex, Plato. They stay instead to the simple beauty of his changeless world of Forms. Thus, most who teach Plato concentrate on the Ideal Republic, and ignore the forces that lead to its deterioration, which he in fact describes in detail.

"...violence and destruction were the most powerful stimulants to his [Dickens'] imagination,"[6] Carey reports. Thus,

---

[4] Ibid., p28.
[5] Ibid., p10.
[6] Ibid., p.16.

imagination and creativity, which are so volatile and explosive, become "real" for the metaphysics of the 21st century, as every morning newspaper and police report attests. But again, so do comedy and contradiction and laughter become real and important forces in our new "brave new world." "It is characteristic of Dickens's mind that he is able to see almost everything from two opposing points of view,"[7] Carey tells us.

Our logic may be perfect, and some of our ideas can even be made clear and distinct. We may work every theoretical plan out with perfect consistency, but if we lack a sense of humor about our philosophical constructs, a sense of the absurdities in human behavior and about the power of violence and destruction to disrupt "the best laid plans of mice and men," then tragedy awaits us in the future that exists outside the mind's ability to dream pure plots. In order to create and to keep mental balance, an active imagination is key. We need more comedy, a greater sense of every human absurdity in our 21st century play-scripts, if the actors in our drama are to be human beings and not computers. Dickens is essentially a comic writer, which makes his literature still great today just because science has not changed human nature all that much.

What qualities will make our leading figures "great" in the 21st century? To be great always demands an attention to the novelty present in your time. Marx became great because he foresaw and then embodied in thought a coming force in his era. Yet in spite of our attempts to write history in advance, it tends more to write itself out of a massive chaos that challenges us still to respond creatively. "What makes him [Dickens] unique," Carey reports, "is the power of his imagination and, in Kafka's phrase, its 'great, careless, prodigality!'"[8] Then, philosophy, theology, political theory should in the 21st century all come back closer to the art of literature and seek out the power of comedy.

Carey says of Thackery that "perhaps his prodigality was rooted in his self-doubt"[9] In the 17th to 20th centuries we saw the emergence of complete human self-assurance. Descartes wanted a system that removed all doubt, Spinoza one that controlled or

---

[7] Ibid., p.15.
[8] Ibid., p. 7.
[9] Carey, John; Thakery Prodigal Genius, p.9

•

eliminated all emotion. But what if self-doubt is the very origin of imagination and also a needed spur to talent? If it were not so, why the suicide of immensely talented performers, why drug addiction and the nervousness of serious professionals every time the curtain goes up on another public performance? It is not the case that the most talented have the least doubt, but rather more often that the least talented exhibit the greatest surface arrogance. Of course, as any suffering singer, actor, or writer will report, self-doubt can kill productivity too. Our ability to counter doubt's natural intrusion becomes our chief source of unstifled imagination.

Those who live with the young, any teacher or any instructor, know that his or her greatest task and most needed talent is to try to build confidence in students who are both burdened and yet gifted by their talent. As students, they cannot yet have built up any confidence in themselves that rests on solid ground, although cockiness and arrogance often come easily to the young as a substitute for accomplishment. How to negotiate the treacherous and life-threatening passage from the unfocused talent to the disciplined and self-focused product--that is for both teacher and novice "The Great Unknown". Surely more talent is lost or wasted or never gains focus than what manages finally to cross over the gulf to creative production.

Carey reports that Thackery was destroyed by success, so we know we are not allowed to be overly romantic about those who do pass over the bridge from vague stirrings to a final productivity. The same forces of doubt, those which threatened all chance of success, still lie within the person on the other side of the gulf, just because success can blind anyone to the precarious nature of imagination, that is, to its constant closeness to blindness and self-destruction. Milton took any orthodoxy as a starting point for dissent, but then finally he was himself, ironically, made the into epitome of orthodoxy. So you cannot become creative by imitating one who has already become creative, because they did not become innovative by imitating. One must discern how their creativity managed to achieve the forms which we now so admire.

One thing we need to ask is why the Modern World so completely rejected all mysticism, when it is so clear that our poets verge on mysticism and that most creative insight in religion stems from the mystic's talent. The answer seems to be that clarity and finality and certainty were the Modern Age's unchallenged metaphysical assumptions: that now, at last, they could achieve finality in theory. So today, as that Era of the Hope for Finality closes out, the uncertainty and the emotion involved in all literary creation and artistic production becomes a much more realistic metaphysical base for us to assume while entering the 21st century. Imagination can neither be confined nor left uncontrolled, and certainly we can never know in advance which imaginative suggestions may prove insightful--until the chaos of life has tested each one. Complexity, risk, and chance are our New Age's hallmarks, not clarity and finality.

Does all this mean that, contrary to the Enlightenment's noble aims, we cannot lift ourselves from darkness and create a better human world? No, not at all. But it should be clear to us that either to remake whole societies or to secure ourselves against all loss is a dream now "gone with the wind." And more important: evil has not departed and can still reappear in senseless destruction anywhere at any time. It is the shadow side of us all, as Jung pointed out, not some temporary intruder we can now hope to ban. "Progress" is not a lost cause, but we never do leave our past for a higher level certain never to return. Darwin has taught us about our origins, and any divinity who would use such a wasteful, dangerous and terror-filled process in order to get humanity to a conscious state did not, could not, have intended to offer us either the best of all possible worlds or irreversible progress. Our punishment does not fit our crime in Eden.

At all times we live close to our terror-filled origins and bear the signs of our lowly origin always with us; primitive behavior is but a miss-step away. So how will creativity and imagination help us where the advance of the physical sciences could not? Cultures are many and various, but not all are equally desirable or equally conducive to the development of human talents. Inconsistencies in the human drama, which some hoped to remove permanently, are also symptomatic of a flexibility which is vital to the imaginative writer-artist-philosopher-theologian. Thus, if rapid response to change and a willingness to venture into the Age of Exploration of the Worlds Within our Minds, and in all of our souls, the quality of constant flexibility and comedy's revelation of human absurdity--these can be the key to achieving momentary self-control in the 21st century. Darkness and terror and destruction lie latent within us, forever threatening. But this does not mean that we cannot develop some flexible external and internal controls-- and sustain them for at least some time interval.

Postscript II

John Carey has been helpful in our attempt to understand how human imagination operates in literary construction. Let us see if his investigation of John Donne's Art can help us in our project to understand how imagination relates to the discovery of truth.

Carey tells us that Donne was a "transformer of everything" and so is accused by his critics of destroying the ornament of poetry and replacing it with "metaphysical ideas." Given the notion of the scholar who reports to other scholars by using copious footnotes and is then appraised for his or her accuracy, certainly Donne's is a different approach. But of course the basic question we need to decide is whether in fact philosophy lies closer to his metaphysical transformative powers and, in particular, whether truth itself can be discovered in the act of, and in the art of, such transformation.

Another key question appears when Carey tells us that we need to explore "the structure of his [Donne's] imagination and see what makes it individual."[10] This question is crucial because the Modern World, from Descartes to Hegel and particularly later in Marxist doctrine, always sought the universal. They took their lead from the supposed universality which they saw emerging in scientific theory. It is amazing that, although each thinker differed in approach,

---

[10] John Carey. John Donne. <u>Life, Mind, and Art</u>. Faber and Faber: London, 1990, ix.

the necessity of modern philosophy to seek universality was uniformly assumed.   Whatever may be true about stars and atoms, even if the theories about them never achieved universality and finality, could it be that philosophical truth, where humanity is concerned, is forever individual in approach just because insight comes only to individuals and not to ages or societies or even to churches?   What if in philosophy we may have insights but that their arrival requires first our inspiration, which the Greeks often prayed for as they began to speak, and that imagination, crucial as it may be, is always individual and never universal?   As individuals we may appropriate one or more insights from others and still never reach universality in our judgments.

Perhaps, then, continuity in theory depends on imagination which can work to sustain its power but cannot transfer it to any or to all.   Phrases grow out of the continuity of the imaginative process, but still the phrases which philosophers seek stem only from individual imagination.   Carey reports that Donne attaches himself to doctrines not as religious truth but, instead, as imaginative choices.   If so, should both religious doctrines and philosophical truths be agreed to rest on our imaginative choices?   Then they could not be used as an occasion to deride or to slaughter anyone, since all truth must be reached by individual approach.   "...individual decision in the matter are bound, in the end, to rest on the psychological preferences of the believer [or unbeliever]: that is to say, on the structures of his personality and imagination."[11]

If a writer's religious beliefs provide a guide to the workings of his or her fancy, we must understand the workings of imagination if we want to understand the human truth which can be made accessible to us.   Carey tells us that "Donne picked out ideas because he was interested in the feeling they gave."[12]   This might not be all that is needed to produce truth in chemistry, but it could have a great deal to do with the imaginative construction of a new theory, whether human or chemical.   Philosophers have been split either by their rejection of or by their inclusion of feeling in our search for truth.   Yet oddly, imagination seems to require emotion as a base.

---

[11] Ibid., p.xiv.
[12] Ibid., p.xiv.

Let us take some key concepts which Carey focuses on and see if, as he analyses their function in Donne's imaginative mind, they help us to understand how truth should be approached, once the Modern Age's illusion of universalism and finality are gone.[13]

1.) Apostasy

"Donne was born into terror, and formed by it." (p.4).

We thought terror would be eliminated by the coming of democracy and scientific thought. Instead, we find ourselves surrounded by terror as the 21st century approaches. The Enlightenment and Rationalism should have eliminated terror, could they have extended their views universally. Yet as terror returns we have to ask if, at the very least, it can spur our imagination, destructive as it still is.

"...that healing distortion of the truth with which fiction always rewards its creators." (p.24) We thought empirical truth and scientific advance would heal us. Now, we see final truth escaping our grasp, we need to ask what part fiction might play again in our healing, which is so much more needed once terror has returned on a world-wide scale.

"...Donne always allows himself to imagine a state beyond betrayal." (p.24)

We have been betrayed so many times in our Utopian expectations that we need to find a way to imagine ourselves beyond betrayal, that act which has become so much a part of the Late Modern Scene and which was so little expected. How can we go through betrayal and move beyond it? Perhaps the recovery of imagination alone will today allow us to step forward.

2.) Ambition

There is little other than ambition, it would seem, that we should put further from the search for truth. The Moderns liked to think of the truth-seeker as being dispassionate. Yet Donne's major theme is our disjunction from God and the resulting struggle to deal with this. Thus, we need to ask: Is it only Reason which can overcome the divine-human disjunction, which was assumed and which certainly

---

[13] All footnotes in the following sections are from the same volume.

has become a major problem at the end of the 20th century; or can religious passion and faith, so much set aside by Modern thinkers, alone overcome such separation?   Donne's powerful sense of singularity both prompted and prohibited the total union of which he dreamed. Thus, if singularity and an individual approach to truth return, the kind of total union which the utopians dreamed of cannot be achieved as long as individuality remains the path to truth.

> "Donne's art... expresses his personality self -advancing, averous, unsatisfied..." (p.80)

So we must ask if the ambition present in the person may be the key as to whether insight can be achieved. If truth for us is not universal and neutral, the ambition of the seeker may not be a block but rather provide him with a key. What we require in a writer, Carey concludes, "...is not amiability but the power to show us alternative ways of expressing the world." (Ibid.)   Thus, even if they are destructive at times, power and ambition may be linked. But they are also not disconnected from the ability to show us how to express the world in alternate ways-- that prime task of imagination.

Donne did not think he knew himself fully, as Descartes thought both possible and necessary. If the self remains "the hardest object of sight," then truth may take on different forms and so will require different approaches, since some thought the transparent self could be the very touchstone of our certainty (e.g., Descartes). If this is not to be, logic is irrelevant "to the muddled, earnest strivings of the ego." (p.85) In fact, Donne was able easily to leave mere fact behind (that special touchstone of Empiricism) and "head for the stratosphere." (p. 87)

Is it possible, then, that the truth we seek about ourselves is further from, rather than closer to, mere fact? This does not mean that we ignore facts and should not constantly test them. But it may mean that the truth we discover about ourselves does not lie waiting out there, or in there, for us to discover either in some concept or in some set of facts.

3.) Bodies

However, Carey reminds us, as we seek to leave fact behind, that Donne found it a necessity "...to anchor abstract truths in the human anatomy." (p. 121) This is not a denial of "mere fact" but simply highlights our need to make what is abstract connect to our physicality. Remember that Descartes could never find a satisfactory link between mind and body. Could this be just because his mind and his ideas were unreal in their clarity? Perhaps Donne teaches us to head for the stratosphere but then to return and to anchor what we have seen to physicality. Donne felt that the fragmented state of his being actually fired his imagination. So perhaps the finality we moderns claimed to achieve actually crippled our imagination. Donne had a need to focus the powers of his soul "to bring them to unity" (p. 155). But we have to ask: What produces unity? And quite possibly it may be that neither science nor reason accomplishes this but only individual imaginative powers, that is, if "...the self is by nature undiscoverable." (p. 156) His doubts about himself made it necessary to imprint himself on his poems, whereas the Moderns had thought clarity about the self would empower the mind and impel it to abstractions which were universally transferable. But this cannot be so, if in fact the unified self is primarily an imaginative product.

4.) Reason

The Rationalists had sought to find in reason a unity and finality for truth. Donne's arguments "...are frivolous, envious or self-contradictory by turns, but they are almost never genuinely argumentative." (p. 217) Then, Reason may not be the sole instrument to discover truth but more a flexible poetic accessory. You say, that is fine for poetry, but what about philosophical truth? Reason is for Donne "...an agitated facade through which he projects the desires and inconsistencies of his poetic self." (p.217)

This is "the mask of reason," as it has been called, and Aristotle long ago taught us that truth is not the same in every area of our inquiries. We simply thought, with Science and the coming of the Modern World, that truth in all areas would become uniform. Yet perhaps our poetic self is more important to our discovery than we had thought. Like Hume, Carey sees Donne's arguments as being in the service of his will. "What is odd about his poems," Carey reports, "is that they retain a relentless passion for arguing, yet treat argument with patent disrespect." (p.217) Perhaps Donne (and Blake) see truth as a product of individual inspiration rather than as arising from any rational universality.

The issue: Is 'reality' not empirical, that is, where truths concerning ourselves are concerned, while reason may function on the basis of data? But reason fails us if the truth we need to know is not finally grounded in and produced by the empirical/accessible world alone. Donne finds paradoxes everywhere, and for him these do not advance the universal dialectic, as Hegel hoped they would, but actually block it. For those of a Modern persuasion, this would seem to lead to skepticism, as it does for Hume. But Donne sees it in another way. "...skepticism could be liberating as well as mournful..." (p.222) Donne was able to feel of two minds about almost anything, but he exploited its gaiety and dashed hopes rather than seeing the erosion of the Modern dream as "gloom." He loves insoluble paradoxes, which allow us to feel an emancipating power. Why? Because we are released from an unyielding conviction and seriousness. Thus, Comedy returns to us with the 21st century. Not at all because everything turns out according to some Utopian dream, but only because we once again recognize inescapable human foibles. We can laugh at ourselves-- and at the Modern World-- at long last.

5.) Corners

Donne loved corners. They were the meeting place of opposites. Their nature is simultaneously single and double. They stand apart from the simple and the natural which were the key goals for the Modern World. But now Donne leads us to ask: What if the intellectual world for humans (whatever is it for science) is by nature singular vs. universal? This finding stands apart from the supposed simplicity of the Natural world, which Empiricism hoped to use as a model. "Division fascinated him as much as union." (p. 27)

What pleases the imagination is not coalescence but rather opposites striving within union, "of paired antagonists locked together." (Ibid.) For a moment this might sound like Hegel, but remember that no Universal Reason governs all this nor does it lead to Progress. It has a closer link to the loss and terror of Darwin's world-outlook. All is not total chaos; there is just a never ending aspect to our pursuits. "The farthest West is East, where the West never ends, the East begins." (p. 250) He does not say, as some have, that never the twain shall meet. It is just that we move in seamless transition from one to another and back again. There is a connecting and compacting tendency which Carey notes in all Donne's thought and poetry. So the corners that he loved must be dealt with. They are the endless challenge and proof of the non-finality of all thought.

But "...the mysterious junction of body and soul lies at the heart of Donne's obsession with merging." (p. 263) Remember that Descartes had trouble linking body and soul. He thought the mind capable of final clarity, partly because he saw God as the epitome of clarity. Donne return to mystery, because the soul never becomes fully and finally clear, and God lies beyond our final rational appropriation. Yet it is the connection of body and soul that lies at the heart of the mystery which now re-enters human thought. In such a case, poetry may be able to express such truth with greater power. Mystery may actually inspire imagination, not inhibit it as the Modern World thought, and which had prompted both their desire for a final clarity and their obsession to eliminate all mystery.

In our own time, the nature of truth as uncertain, plus the power and the limits on all Reason, have never been more prominent or raised more questions. If universalism has fled along with the Modern World at least where our self-comprehension is concerned, then the singularity of human vision need not be a block in our approach to truth In fact, it is perhaps our last best hope or avenue. "Power to the people"-- to those who can accept uncertainty, plus the restriction imposed by our human limitations, and who can appreciate the singularity of vision-- when and wherever imaginative insight appears.

Postscript III: On 'Reality' and It's Creation

If we are considering 'truth' and 'imagination' and their relationship, we must ask the ancient but still pertinent metaphysical question: What is 'Reality' and can it be apprehended (if not comprehended) in varying degrees? Also: If the Empiricists started with a wrong assumption about locating reality in sense experience, and if the Rationalists thought they had found a firm reality by the use of Reason, what is the 'Reality' we might find by the use of our human imagination? And more important, if we do discover a much overlooked (by philosophers at least) mode of Reality by the use of imagination, how does this relate to our other human experiences of empirical and psychological reality and so provide us with a key to understanding 'Reality' as a whole?

Let us listen to John Beer as he comments on Blake: "Where does the poet derive the 'reality' in which his art is founded? From the world about him, or from the structuring of his own inward vision."[14] Philosophers need not be Empiricists or Rationalists or Idealists, although they certainly may be, since the approach, their basic assumption of where Reality lies and of where truth is to be found, defines the philosopher and shapes his or her questions, if not the answers given as well. However, philosophers have an ancient

---

[14] Beer, John. Blake's Humanism. Barnes and Noble: New York, 1968, p.8.
All page numbers in this section are to this volume.

right to refuse to offer to others any "answers" to the questions which they raise for them.

Again, Beer notes Blake's revolutionary approach which may now have come to define us all in the pre-21st century, except for the slavish followers of theoretical fads: "Once he revolted against the world-picture of his time he must build a world-picture of his own..." (p.10) The philosopher and the poet, then, are (or should be) born theoretical revolutionaries. To adopt the accepted theories of reality of the day is to show one's poetic insensitivity and one's philosophical naiveté. Marx, Hegel and a host of others of the Modern Persuasion thought Reality could be brought into one focus and then into finality and so perhaps into our control. But if it was the rise Modern Science that led us into this optimism-of-finality, it is also the explosion of scientific-theoretical speculation which has led us to a new Reality characterized more by theoretical plurality and so by non-finality.

Of course, the great hope of the Modern Vision was that we could be made happy by theoretical finality. But in point of fact, if we had to characterize our mood of passage into the 21st century, it is one of widespread unhappiness even among many who possess material plenty. We ask: Is what unites the halves and the have-nots of our time a lack of vision? "...he [Blake] saw that men are made unhappy not only by lack of bread but by lack of vision." (p.206) If so, Marx's materialism represents a fundamental failure to appraise that level of Reality which is perhaps most important to human beings, our imaginative visions, individual as these must be. The implication: We should not fail to provide bread for all, but we must always offer the vision of alternative futures as well.

Still, those in economic poverty or in physical distress have basic human needs which must be provided for by any society which calls itself "civilized" (is that not the very meaning of 'civilization?'). But as simple human beings of all races and creeds, what do we require for our satisfaction? Could it be that, beyond basic subsistence, new visions are our key need? "Where there is no vision the people perish." And such new light can come neither from sense experience nor from reason. Visions are of different origins. And these depend on, and so can lead us to, what we are willing to label as 'Reality.' Because, if we disparage visions we are all condemned to a pedestrian existence. Do the poor, once their basic bread is provided, need vision more than they need cake? It could be, since our basic need is to envision something beyond a squalid existence.

Many stress 'Nature' today, and it is important to keep close to our natural environment. But is it the case that we far overstress the importance of raw Nature to us, in spite of the fact that we should not violate it by pollution? Beer reports that "Blake distrusts nature as soon as it ceased to be formed by vision." (p.211) So could it be that, as much as we need to celebrate and protect 'Nature' today, in itself it is not as important as to have a vision which informs both our treatment of it and of ourselves? If then, Nature is there but is always of secondary importance for our spiritual health, we can have all we want of physical plenty about us, or only a minimum natural sustenance, and still be happy if informed by a vision. 'Reality,' then, is not strictly 'natural' or universal but rather still largely unseen in any day or by any person. The excitement of such an adventure to locate our Reality ultimately is what drives us on.

Freud, we know, stresses our memory and our need to discover its role in our psychological healing. But what if it is the case that "imagination has nothing to do with memory." (p.919) This means that Hume's exploration of memory, plus the short-comings of any Empiricism based on the present, are both quite crucial. Thus, the Freudian who takes us back to our childhood is headed in a right direction--at first at least. Our difficulties may lie in a past that is in need of reconciliation. But if we detach memory from insight, we can only try to discover our guilt in a physical fact, Blake repeatedly reports to us. If so, the discovery of Blake's reliance on imagination might be reduced to those who become computer experts.

We tend to think that our main problem of liberty lies with those who have developed arguments about political theory and human rights. Political liberty is but a first human need. Even if liberty is achieved politically, it could be brought into existence and still not have "my future in mind." Blake tells us that liberty can be established, even if it is not political in appearance. Those who lead us in our public projects should all feel the need to admire Blake for his imagination. He suggests that the volume of our achievements are in ready supply. In democracies our dreams are moving in the right direction--just we often do not realize that they are not totally politically dependent.

Hunger is certainly real. A beautiful body- or spirit- is real, all so much so that we are often driven to target these as our primary obsessions. The momentary vision of a "Ten" can be more real than any rock, however brief it is, but there is no question that God is real and powerful and that Art is vivid also. We should neither neglect the Art we have achieved nor what still exists only in our speculations. Given such a vision of "Reality," we should begin by assuming that Art stirs us to move ahead with its claims to see visions of utopias that can drive us on-- even if they are not destined for factual reality.

We continue to search for 'truth,' but all the while it lies within the very structures of our imagination, which seems to able to balance itself on a small insight. Nevertheless, our calculations of the future tend to pass out of our control, as 'Reality' does too. Why? Because imagination helps us to locate truth, much more so than either sensation or reason. They tend to limit us; imagination tends to expand. Reason seeks universal agreement; imagination is of necessity individual, which makes it as necessary for our intellectual health as it is hard to appraise even after it arrives. Reality-for-us is not as obvious in its location as the Modern World hoped. Thus, we must follow the inspired individual, whether or not he or she sometimes proves to be a false guide, since this is not ascertainable in advance of our attempt to create new insights into Reality for the common good.

Our guiding words for the New Century might be these:

"Whence does a poet derive the 'reality' in which his art is founded? From the world about him, or from the structuring of his own inward vision?"[15]

"Once he revolted against the world-picture of his time he must build a world-picture of his own..." (p.12).

"...he [Blake] saw that men are made unhappy not by lack of bread but by lack of vision." (p.206).

---

[15] Beer, John. Blake's Humanism. Barnes and Noble: New York, 1968, p.8. All quotes that follow are from this volume.

"Blake...distrusts nature as soon as it ceases to be informed by vision."   (p.211).

"Imagination has nothing to do with memory." (p.212)

"If liberty could not be achieved politically, it could be brought about in the cultivation of art." (p.223)

INDEX

Other Works by Frederick Sontag

Divine Perfection: Possible Ideas of God, 1962

The Existentialist Prolegomena: To a Future Metaphysics, 1969

*The Future of Theology: A Philosophical Basis for Contemporary
    Protestant Theology, 1969*

The Crisis of Faith: An Argument from the Existence of the Devil, 1970

God, Why Did You Do That?, 1970

The Problems of Metaphysics, 1970

*How Philosophy Shapes Theology: Problems in the Philosophy of
    Religion, 1971*

*The American Religious Experience: The Roots, Trends and the Future of
    American Theology (with John K. Roth), 1972*

Love Beyond Pain: Mysticism Within Christianity, 1977

Sun Myung Moon and the Unification Church, 1977

God and America's Future (with John K. Roth), 1977

What can God Do?, 1979

A Kierkegaard Handbook, 1979

The Elements of Philosophy, 1984

The Questions of Philosophy (with John K. Roth), 1988

Emotion: Its Role in Understanding and Decision, 1989

*The Return of the Gods: A Philosophical/Theological Reappraisal of the
    Works of Ernest Becker, 1989.*

Uncertain Truth, 1995

Wittgenstein and the Mystical, 1995

The Acts of the Trinity, 1996

Descent of Woman, 1997